Nic

iPad
for Seniors

13th edition
covers all versions of iPad with iPadOS 17
(including iPad mini and iPad Pro)

In easy steps is an imprint of In Easy Steps Limited
16 Hamilton Terrace · Holly Walk · Leamington Spa
Warwickshire · United Kingdom · CV32 4LY
www.ineasysteps.com

Thirteenth Edition

Notice of Liability
Every effort has been made to ensure that this book
contains accurate and current information. However, In
Easy Steps Limited and the author shall not be liable for
any loss or damage suffered by readers as a result of
any information contained herein.

Trademarks
iPad® is a registered trademark of Apple Computer, Inc.
All other trademarks are acknowledged as belonging to
their respective companies.

In Easy Steps Limited supports The Forest Stewardship
Council (FSC), the leading international forest
certification organization. All our titles that are printed
on Greenpeace approved FSC certified paper carry the
FSC logo.

FSC
www.fsc.org

MIX
Paper from
responsible sources
FSC® C020837

Printed and bound in the United Kingdom

ISBN 978-1-78791-006-5

Contents

1 Choosing your iPad

It's compact, it's stylish, it's powerful; and it's perfect for anyone, of any age. This chapter introduces the iPad, its different models, the iPadOS 17 operating system and its interface, and some of the basic controls and functions so that you can quickly get up and running with your new iPad.

"Apps" is just a fancy name for what are more traditionally called programs in the world of computing. The iPad has several apps that come built in and ready for use. There are thousands more available to download from the online App Store (see Chapter 5).

The **NEW** icon pictured above indicates a new or enhanced feature introduced with iPads using iPadOS 17.

The iEverything

The iPad is a tablet computer that has gone a long way to change how we think of computers and how we interact with them. Instead of a large, static object it is effortlessly mobile, and even makes a laptop seem bulky by comparison.

But even with its compact size, the iPad still manages to pack a lot of power and functionality into its diminutive body. In this case, small is most definitely beautiful, and the range of what you can do with the iPad is considerable:

● Communicate via email, video and text messaging.

● Surf the web wirelessly.

● Add an endless number of new "apps" from the Apple App Store.

● Use a range of entertainment tools covering music, photos, videos, books and games.

● Do all of your favorite productivity tasks such as word processing, creating spreadsheets or producing presentations.

● Organize your life with apps for calendars, address books, notes, reminders, and much more.

Add to this up to 10 hours' battery life when you are on the move, a range of different sizes (with a Retina Display screen of outstanding clarity) and a seamless backup system, and it is clear why the iPad can stylishly fulfill all of your computing needs.

Simplicity of the iPad

Computers have become a central part of our everyday lives, but there is no reason why they need to be complex devices that have us scratching our heads as to how to best use them. The iPad is not only stylish and compact; it also makes the computing process as simple as possible so that you can concentrate on what you want to do. Some ways in which this is done are:

- **Quickly on**. With the iPad, there is no long wait for it to turn on or wake from a state of sleep. When you turn it on, it is ready to use; it's as simple as that.

- **Apps**. iPad apps sit on the Home screen, visible and ready to use. Most apps are created in a similar format, so once you have mastered getting around them you will be comfortable using the majority of them.

- **Settings**. One of the built-in iPad apps is Settings. This is a one-stop shop for customizing the way that your iPad looks and operates, and also how settings for apps work.

The Dock is the bar at the bottom of the iPad screen, onto which apps can be placed for quick access.

Much of the way you navigate around the iPad is done by tapping or swiping with your fingers, rather than with a traditional keyboard and mouse. There is also a virtual keyboard for input functions.

- **Dock and App Switcher window**. These are two functions that enable you to access your favorite apps quickly, regardless of what you are doing on your iPad.

- **Home button**. This enables you to return to the main Home screen at any time. It also has some additional functionality, depending on how many times you click it.

Some iPad models do not have a **Home** button and use the top button (**On/Off**) on the body of the iPad to perform some of these functions.

Models and Sizes

Since its introduction in 2010, the iPad has evolved in both its size and specifications. It is now a family of devices, rather than a single size. When choosing your iPad, the first consideration is which size to select. There are four options:

- **iPad**. This is the original version of the iPad, and retains the standard iPad title. Its high-resolution Liquid Retina Display screen measures 10.9 inches (diagonal).

At the time of printing, the latest version is the 10th generation of the standard-size iPads, which have a storage capacity of either 64 gigabytes (GB) or 256GB and use the A14 Bionic chip for processing. The latest version of the iPad supports using the Apple Pencil and the new Magic Keyboard Folio (early versions of the iPad can use the Smart Keyboard). All keyboards and Apple Pencils are bought separately – see pages 14-15 for more details. The Magic Keyboard Folio and the Smart Keyboard have a Smart Connector to attach them, and this ensures that they work as soon as they are attached, without the need for any cables. The Apple Pencil has to be "paired" with the iPad, which involves opening **Settings** > **Bluetooth** and turning Bluetooth **On**. Then, attach the Apple Pencil via the Lightning Connector. It should then be paired and ready for use. The 10th-generation iPad does not have a **Home** button and uses a Touch ID sensor for unlocking the iPad. This is incorporated into the **On/Off** button, and Touch ID can be set up in the same way as for the **Home** button that is available on earlier models of iPads – see page 23 for details about setting up Touch ID.

Don't forget

Another variation in the iPad family is how they connect to the internet and online services. This is with either just Wi-Fi connectivity or Wi-Fi and 5G/4G connectivity (where available, but it also covers 3G). This should be considered if you need to connect to the internet with a cellular connection when you are traveling away from home. 5G, 4G and 3G enable you to connect to a mobile network to access the internet, in the same way as with a cell/mobile phone. This requires a contract with a provider of this type of service.

Don't forget

In October 2023, Apple announced a USB-C version of the Apple Pencil, for this type of connector.

- **iPad Air**. This is similar to the standard iPad, but with a 10.5-inch display. However, it is the thinnest of the iPad models, at 6.1 mm, and supports use of the Apple Pencil, the Magic Keyboard, and the Smart Keyboard Folio. At the time of printing, the latest model of the iPad Air is the 5th generation.

- **iPad mini**. The iPad mini is similar in most respects to the larger versions, except for its size. The screen is 8.3 inches (diagonal) and it weighs slightly less than the iPad and iPad Air. The iPad mini has a Liquid Retina Display screen. The latest version, at the time of printing, is the 6th-generation iPad mini, and it supports use of the Apple Pencil.

Hot tip

The iPad mini is an excellent option for carrying around in a bag or a large pocket.

...cont'd

Face ID can be set up for the iPad Pro in **Settings** > **Face ID & Passcode**.

At the time of printing, Stage Manager is only available on a limited number of iPad models: iPad Air (5th generation), iPad Pro 12.9-inch (3rd generation and later), and iPad Pro 11-inch (1st generation and later). Stage Manager can be accessed from the Control Center, by tapping once on this button:

- **iPad Pro**. This is the most powerful iPad and is an excellent option for all computing and productivity tasks. At the time of printing, the latest model is the 6th generation, which comes with a 12.9-inch screen.

Some earlier versions, 4th generation and earlier, also have a model with an 11-inch screen or a 10.5-inch screen. The latest iPad Pro has a range of options, with storage capacity of 128GB, 256GB, 512GB, 1 terabyte (TB) or 2TB. It uses the powerful Apple M2 chip for fast processing and Face ID for unlocking the screen (it does not have a **Home** button). The iPad Pro can be used with the Magic Keyboard and the Smart Keyboard Folio. It also supports use of the Apple Pencil. The iPad Pro 6th generation also supports **Stage Manager**. This is a function that can be used to minimize

currently-open apps at the left-hand side of the screen, leaving the active app in the center of the screen. To access one of the other apps, tap on it in the left-hand sidebar and it becomes the active one.

Specifications Explained

Most models of iPad have the same range of specifications (the main difference being the screen sizes). Some specifications to consider are:

- **Processor**: This determines the speed at which the iPad operates and how quickly tasks are performed.

- **Storage**: This determines how much content can be stored on the iPad. Across the iPad family, the range is 64GB, 128GB, 256GB, 512GB, 1TB or 2TB.

- **Connectivity**: The options for this are Wi-Fi and 5G/4G/3G connectivity for the internet, and Bluetooth for connecting to other devices over short distances.

- **Cameras**: The front-facing camera is a FaceTime one, which is best for video calls or "selfies" (self-portraits). The back-facing camera is a high-resolution one that takes excellent photos and videos.

- **Screen**: iPads that can run iPadOS 17 all have Retina Display screens for the highest resolution and best clarity. This is an LED-backlit screen.

- **Operating system**: The latest version of the iPad operating system is iPadOS 17.

- **Battery power**: This is the length of time the iPad can be used for general use, such as surfing the web on Wi-Fi, watching video, or listening to music. All models offer approximately 10 hours of use in this way.

- **Input/Output**: These include a Lightning Connector port (for charging), 3.5 mm stereo headphone minijack, built-in speaker, microphone and nano-SIM card tray (Wi-Fi and 5G/4G/3G model only).

- **Sensors**: These are used to determine the amount of ambient light and also the orientation in which the iPad is being held. The sensors include an accelerometer, an ambient light sensor, a barometer and a gyroscope.

The amount of storage you need may change once you have bought your iPad. If possible, buy a version with as much as possible, as you cannot add more later.

Some iPad models have a USB-C Connector, rather than a Lightning Connector. These include: iPad Pro 11-inch (2nd generation and later), iPad Pro 12.9-inch (3rd generation and later), iPad Air (4th generation and later), and iPad mini (6th generation and later). This is used for charging the iPad and it can also be used to connect a USB-C flashdrive and external devices using USB-C.

Hot tip

In October 2023, Apple announced a USB-C version of the Apple Pencil, for this type of connector.

Hot tip

The Apple Pencil can be used to annotate PDF documents or screenshots simply by writing on them. This is known as **Instant Markup**. To annotate a screenshot, press and hold the **On/Off** button and **Home** button simultaneously to capture the screenshot (for iPads without a **Home** button, press and hold the **On/Off** button and the **Volume up** button, and then release them simultaneously). A thumbnail of the screenshot appears in the bottom left-hand corner for a few seconds. Tap once on this to expand it, and use the drawing tools at the bottom of the screen to annotate it.

Apple Pencil

The Apple Pencil is a stylus that can be used on the screen instead of your finger to perform a variety of tasks. At the time of printing, the latest version of the Apple Pencil is the Apple Pencil 2nd generation, although this is only compatible with a more limited range of newer iPads. The Apple Pencil can be used for the following:

- Drawing intricate (or simple) artwork using drawing or painting apps.

- Moving around web pages by swiping or tapping on links to access other web pages.

- Selecting items of text by tapping on them and also dragging the selection handles.

- Annotating PDF documents.

Charging the Apple Pencil

The Apple Pencil can be charged using the iPad Lightning Connector port (the same one as for charging the iPad) or the iPad's charging cable, using the Apple Pencil's Lightning adapter, which is supplied with the Apple Pencil.

To check the level of Apple Pencil charge, swipe from left to right on the Home screen to access the Today View panel (see page 35) and swipe down to the **Batteries** section (and also view the level of charge for the iPad).

📱 Nick's iPad	79%	🔋
✏️ Apple Pencil	37%	⚡🔋

Keyboards

Although the virtual keyboard on the iPad (see Chapter 4 for details) is excellent for text and data inputting, it is not ideal for longer tasks such as writing a vacation journal. To overcome this, there are now several external Apple keyboards that can be used with the range of iPad models. These connect using the Smart Connector on the iPad and do not require any cables. The keyboards are:

- **Magic Keyboard Folio**. This can be used with the latest version of the standard iPad – the iPad 6th generation. The keyboard includes a trackpad.

- **Magic Keyboard**. This can be used with iPad Pro 12.9-inch (3rd generation and later), iPad Pro 11-inch (1st, 2nd, 3rd, and 4th generations), and iPad Air (4th and 5th generations). The keyboard includes a trackpad.

- **Smart Keyboard Folio**. This can be used with Pad Pro 12.9-inch (3rd generation and later), iPad Pro 11-inch (1st, 2nd, 3rd, and 4th generations), and iPad Air (4th and 5th generations). The keyboard does not include a trackpad.

- **Smart Keyboard**. This can be used with the latest standard iPads (7th, 8th, and 9th generations), iPad Air (3rd generation), and iPad Pro 10.5-inch. The keyboard does not include a trackpad.

Keyboard shortcuts

Some keyboard shortcuts that can be performed on the iPad keyboards are:

- **Command (cmd) + H**: Return to Home screen.

- **Command + Tab**: Access the App Switcher bar, in the middle of the screen. Press the **Tab** button to move through the apps in the App Switcher. Stop at the app you want to open.

- **Command + spacebar**: Access the Spotlight Search.

- **Press and hold Command**: A list of Smart Keyboard shortcuts in specific apps.

If an external keyboard is not used, the virtual one will be available instead.

The iPad keyboards also support standard keyboard shortcuts such as:

Command + C: Copy.

Command + V: Paste.

Command + X: Cut.

Command + Z: Undo.

Command + B: Adds bold to selected text.

Command + I: Adds italics to selected text.

Command + U: Adds underline to selected text.

To turn on the iPad, press and hold the **On/Off** button for a few seconds. It can also be used to sleep the iPad or wake it from the **Sleep** state, by pressing it once.

Some iPad models use the top button (**On/Off**) on the body of the iPad to perform some of the functions of the **Home** button.

If your iPad ever freezes, it can be rebooted by holding down the **Home** button and the **On/Off** button for 10 seconds and then turning it on again by pressing and holding the **On/Off** button. (For some models, the combination is the **On/Off** button and the **Volume** button.)

Before you Switch On

The external controls for the iPad are simple. Three of them are situated at the top of the iPad and the other is in the middle, at the bottom. There are also two cameras – one on the front and one on the back of the iPad.

Controls

The controls at the top of the iPad are:

On/Off button and a touch sensor for unlocking the latest iPhone models.

Cameras. One is located on the back, underneath the **On/Off** button, and one on the front, at the top.

Volume Up and **Down** buttons.

Home button. Press this once to wake up the iPad or return to the Home screen at any point.

Speakers. The speakers are located on the bottom edge of the iPad.

Lightning Connector. Connect the Lightning Connector here to charge the iPad, or connect it to another computer. Some iPad models have a USB-C Connector, rather than a Lightning Connector. These include: iPad Pro 11-inch (2nd generation and later), iPad Pro 12.9-inch (3rd generation and later), iPad Air (4th generation and later), and iPad mini (6th generation and later).

Getting Started

To start using the iPad, hold down the **On/Off** button for a few seconds, after which there will be a series of setup screens. These can include some, or all, of the following:

- **Language** and **Country**. Select a language and country.

- **Quick Start**. This can be used to transfer settings from another compatible device, such as an iPhone.

- **Written and Spoken Languages**. Select languages for keyboards and dictation.

- **Wi-Fi network**. Connect to the internet via Wi-Fi.

- **Data & Privacy**. This is used to identify features that ask for your personal information.

- **Touch ID**. Use this on compatible models to create a Touch ID for unlocking your iPad with a fingerprint (or Face ID for iPads with this functionality).

- **Create a Passcode**. This can be used to create a numerical passcode for unlocking your iPad.

- **Apps & Data**. This can be used to set up an iPad from an iCloud backup, or as a new iPad.

- **Apple ID and iCloud**. This can be used to link to an existing iCloud account or create a new one.

- **Make this your new iPad**. From an iCloud backup, this can be used to set up your iPad as a new one.

- **Keep your iPad Up to Date**. This can be used to install updates to the operating system (iPadOS) automatically.

- **Location Services**. This allows apps to use your current location, such as the Maps app.

- **Siri**. This is used to set up Siri, the digital voice assistant.

- **Screen Time**. This can be used to show how much you use your iPad and to add restrictions.

- **Analytics**. This can be used to send data to Apple.

A lot of the initial settings can be skipped during the setup process and accessed later from the **Settings** app. Some geographical differences could apply to the setup process.

For details about obtaining an Apple ID, see page 99.

To turn off an iPad, press and hold the **On/Off** button until the **slide to power off** screen appears. For iPads without a **Home** button, press and hold the **On/Off** button and one of the **Volume** buttons until the same screen appears.

iPadOS 17 is the latest operating system for the iPad.

iPadOS 17 is not compatible with some older models of iPad but can be run on: iPad 6th generation and later, iPad mini 5th generation and later, iPad Air 3rd generation and later, and all models of iPad Pro, except the 1st-generation 9.7-inch and 12.9-inch models. The iPad model number is on the back of the iPad – visit **https://support.apple. com/en-us/HT201471** to find out which model you have.

To check the version of iPadOS, look in **Settings** > **General** > **Software Update**.

About iPadOS 17

iPadOS 17 is the fourth version of the iPad operating system that is a separate version to the one used on iPhones – iOS. However, although iPadOS 17 has its own designation, it is still very closely aligned to the latest version of iOS (iOS 17). Where iPadOS 17 differs from iOS is in the iPad-specific features, such as enhanced multitasking options. Some of the new features in iPadOS 17 include:

- **Customizing the Lock screen**. This provides numerous design options for customizing the Lock screen. This can include customizing the background, creating your own text styles, and adding various widgets.

- **Messages app Plus button**. This is a feature that provides greater functionality to the Messages app and enables you to access a range of features and content. These include sharing your current location, sending a voice note with a transcription, and creating your own customized stickers that can be added to messages and in other compatible apps.

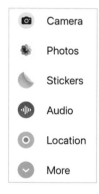

- **Health app**. For the first time, Apple's popular and powerful Health app is included on the iPad, providing access to a considerable range of health and wellbeing data and information. The app can also be synchronized with an iPhone and an Apple Watch.

Home Screen

Once you have completed the setup process, you will see the Home screen of the iPad. This contains the built-in apps and the Home screen widgets (at the top of the screen).

The backgrounds for iPadOS 17 can be changed in **Settings** > **Wallpaper**, or as part of the process for customizing the Lock screen – see pages 42-45.

At the bottom of the screen are seven apps that appear by default in the Dock area (left-hand side) and recently-accessed apps (right-hand side).

Rotate the iPad, and the orientation changes automatically, unless the rotation function has been locked (see page 40).

Items on the Dock can be removed and new ones can be added. For more details, see pages 30-31.

Home Button

The **Home** button, located at the bottom middle of the iPad, can be used to perform a number of tasks.

Some models of iPad use the top button (**On/Off**) on the body of the iPad to perform some of the functions of the **Home** button.

1 Click once on the **Home** button to return to the Home screen at any point

For more details about the App Switcher, see pages 52-53.

2 Double-click on the **Home** button to access the **App Switcher** window. This shows the most recently-used and open apps

Pinch together with thumb and four fingers on the screen to return to the Home screen from any open app.

3 Press and hold on the **Home** button to access Siri, the voice assistant function

For more information about using the iPad search facilities, see pages 58-60.

Opening Items

All apps on your iPad can be opened with minimal fuss and effort. To do this:

 Tap once on an icon to open the app

 The app opens at its own Home screen

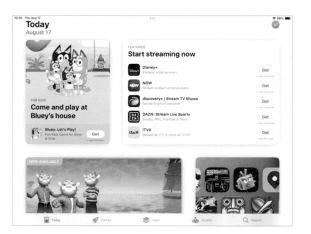

Some models of iPad do not have a physical **Home** button. If this is the case, swipe up from the bottom of the screen to return to the Home screen.

 Click once on the **Home** button to return to the main iPad Home screen

 From the **App Switcher** window, swipe between apps and tap on one to open it directly

For details about using the **App Switcher**, and closing items, see pages 52-53.

Using the Lock Screen

To save power, it is possible to set your iPad screen to lock automatically. This is the equivalent of the **Sleep** option on a traditional computer. To do this:

The screen can also be locked by pressing once on the **On/Off** button.

Notifications can be displayed on the iPad's Lock screen. This can be activated by going to **Settings** > **Notifications** > **Show Previews** and then selecting **Always**. For details about customizing the Lock screen, see pages 42-45.

Once a passcode has been set, tap on the **Require Passcode** button in the **Touch ID & Passcode** section to specify when the passcode is activated. The best option is **Immediately**, to avoid unauthorized access to the iPad.

1   Tap once on the **Settings** app

Settings

2   Tap once on the **Display & Brightness** tab

Display & Brightness

3   Tap once on the **Auto-Lock** option

Auto-Lock   5 minutes >

4   Select a length of time until the iPad is locked automatically, when it is not being used

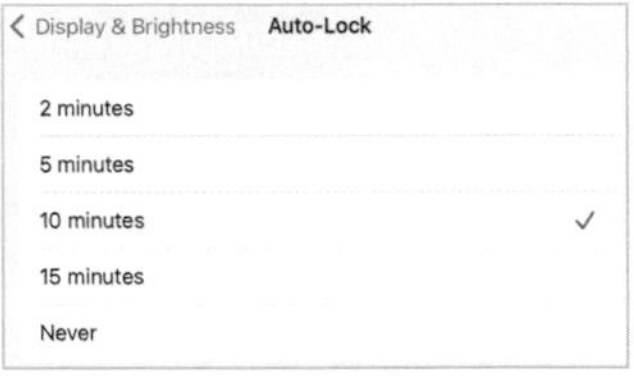

< Display & Brightness   Auto-Lock

2 minutes
5 minutes
10 minutes   ✓
15 minutes
Never

Locking and unlocking an iPad

When the iPad is locked – i.e. the Lock screen is displayed – it can be unlocked simply by pressing the **Home** button (or the **On/Off** button for models without a **Home** button). However, this is not secure, as anyone could unlock the iPad. A better option is to add a numerical passcode. To do this:

1   Select **Settings** > **Touch ID & Passcode**

2   Tap once on the **Turn Passcode On** button

3   By default, enter a 6-digit passcode. This can be used to unlock your iPad from the Lock screen. Confirm the passcode on the next screen. The passcode is now required whenever the iPad is locked

Fingerprint sensor with Touch ID

For greater security, the **Home** button can be used as a fingerprint sensor to unlock your iPad with the unique fingerprint that has set it up. (A passcode also has to be set up in case the Touch ID does not work.) To do this:

1 Select **Settings** > **Touch ID & Passcode**

2 Create a passcode as shown on the previous page (this is required if the fingerprint sensor is unavailable for any reason).
Drag the **iPad Unlock** button **On**

USE TOUCH ID FOR:

iPad Unlock

Wallet & Apple Pay

iTunes & App Store

Password AutoFill

3 Tap once on the **Add a Fingerprint...** link. This presents a screen for creating your Touch ID

FINGERPRINTS

Add a Fingerprint...

4 Place your finger on the **Home** button several times to create a Touch ID. This will include capturing the edges of your finger. The screens move automatically after each part

Place Your Finger

Lift and rest your finger on the Home button repeatedly.

is captured, and the fingerprint icon turns red. Complete the Touch ID wizard to create a unique fingerprint for unlocking your iPad

For iPads without a **Home** button, the **On/Off** button is used for Touch ID. Some models also use Face ID face recognition instead of Touch ID – see page 24.

The fingerprint sensor is very effective, although it may take a bit of practice until you can get the right position for your finger to unlock the iPad first time, every time. It can only be unlocked with the same finger that created the Touch ID in Step 4. Additional fingerprints can also be set up.

A "wizard" is a computer program that guides you through a process.

23

Face ID

For some iPad models, unlocking the iPad is done through the use of Face ID face recognition. If this cannot be used for any reason, a passcode can be entered instead, to unlock the iPad. To set up Face ID:

Don't forget

At the time of printing, the iPads that use Face ID rather than Touch ID are: iPad Pro 11-inch (2nd generation and later) and iPad Pro 12.9-inch (3rd generation and later).

Don't forget

When setting up Face ID a passcode also has to be created, in case the Face ID function does not work for any reason. This is done by tapping once on the **Turn Passcode On** button in the **Face ID & Passcode** section of the Settings app.

1 Select **Settings** > **Face ID & Passcode**

Face ID & Passcode

2 Tap once on the **Set Up Face ID** button and tap once on the **Get Started** button

Set Up Face ID

Get Started

3 Position your face in the center of the circle that accesses the iPad's camera. Move your head slowly in a circle so that the camera can record all elements of your face

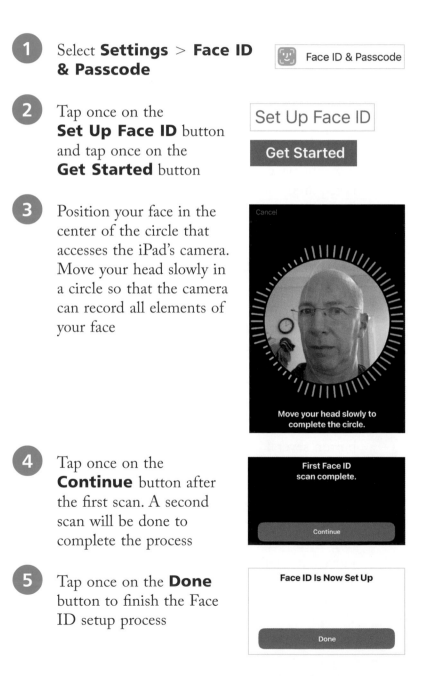

4 Tap once on the **Continue** button after the first scan. A second scan will be done to complete the process

First Face ID scan complete.

Continue

5 Tap once on the **Done** button to finish the Face ID setup process

Face ID Is Now Set Up

Done

2 Around your iPad

Once you have turned on your iPad you will want to start using it as soon as possible. This chapter shows how to do this, with details about: settings; navigation; using the new widgets on the Home screen; accessing the Control Center; customization; multitasking; using notifications; and searching for items.

Don't forget

If a **Settings** option has an **On/Off** button next to it, this can be changed by swiping the button to either the left or right. Green indicates that the option is **On**.

Hot tip

The **Display & Brightness** setting has an option for **Dark Mode**, which inverts the screen, with a dark background and white text. This can make the screen easier to read in certain conditions. To use Dark Mode, tap on the **Dark** button. To specify when Dark Mode is activated, drag the **Automatic** button **On**, or tap once on the **Options** button to specify a time for Dark Mode.

iPad Settings

The **Settings** app controls settings for the appearance of the iPad and the way it and its apps operate:

- **Apple ID, iCloud, Media & Purchases**. This contains settings for items that are to be saved to the online iCloud service (see pages 62-66).

- **Airplane Mode**. This can be used while on an airplane.

- **Wi-Fi**. This enables you to select a wireless network.

- **Bluetooth**. Turn this **On** to connect Bluetooth devices.

- **Notifications**. This determines how the Notification Center operates (see pages 54-55).

- **Sounds**. This has options for setting sounds for alerts.

- **Focus**. Use this to specify times when you do not want to receive, or restrict, calls and notifications.

- **Screen Time**. This is used to view details of your iPad use and add restrictions (see pages 178-180).

- **General**. This contains several commonly-used settings.

- **Control Center**. This determines how the Control Center operates (see pages 38-41).

- **Display & Brightness**. This can be used to set the screen brightness, text size and bold text.

- **Home Screen & App Library**. This has an option for the size of Home screen icons and also the functionality of the App Library.

- **Multitasking & Gestures**. This has options for working with multitasking screen views and how gestures can be used to navigate around your iPad.

- **Accessibility**. This can be used for users with visual or motor issues (see pages 182-186 for details).

- **Wallpaper**. To change the iPad's wallpaper, tap once on the **Add New Wallpaper** option.

- **Siri & Search**. Options for turning on the digital voice assistant, and settings such as language and voice style.

- **Apple Pencil**. This has options for using an Apple Pencil with an iPad.

- **Touch ID & Passcode**. This has options for creating a fingerprint ID for unlocking your iPad (see page 23), or **Face ID & Passcode** (see page 24).

- **Battery**. This shows the battery usage of specific apps and can show the battery level in the status bar.

- **Privacy & Security**. This can be used to activate Location Services so that your location can be used by specific apps.

- **App Store**. This can be used to specify download options for the App Store.

- **Wallet & Apple Pay**. This can be used to set up Apple Pay for online payments.

- **Passwords**. This contains options for managing website passwords.

- **Mail, Contacts, Calendars**. These are three separate settings, with options for how these three apps operate.

iPad app settings

Most of the built-in iPad apps have their own settings that determine how the apps operate. These include: Notes, Reminders, Freeform, Voice Memos, Messages, FaceTime, Safari, News, Stocks, Weather, Translate, Maps, Measure, Shortcuts, Home, Music, TV, Photos, Camera, Books, and Podcasts. Tap on one of these tabs to view the settings for that app. (Apps that are downloaded from the App Store also have their individual settings in this location in the Settings app.)

If you have an iPad with 5G/4G/3G connectivity, there will also be a setting for **Cellular/Mobile Service**.

Tap on this arrow to see additional options:

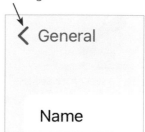

Tap once here to move back to the previous page for the selected setting:

Navigating Around

Much of the navigation on the iPad is done with Multitasking Gestures, which are combinations of tapping, swiping and pinching gestures that can be used to view items such as web pages, photos, maps and documents.

Swiping between screens

Once you have added more apps to your iPad, they will start to fill up more screens. To move between these, swipe left or right with one or two fingers.

Returning to the Home screen

Pinch together with thumb and four fingers to return to the Home screen from any open app, or swipe up from the bottom of the screen. The Home screen can also be accessed by using a long swipe up from the bottom of any screen (a short swipe brings up the Dock, and a slightly longer one brings up the App Switcher).

Swiping up and down

Swipe up and down with one finger to move up or down web pages, photos, maps or documents. The content moves in the opposite direction of the swipe; i.e. if you swipe up, the page will move down, and vice versa.

You can also move between different screens by tapping once on one of the small white dots in the middle of the screen above the Dock, illustrated on page 30.

You can also return to the Home screen by clicking once on the **Home** button, if your iPad has one.

The faster you swipe on the screen, the faster the screen moves up or down.

Tapping and zooming

Double-tap with one finger to zoom in on a web page, photo, map or document. Double-tap with one finger to return to the original view.

Pinching and swiping

Swipe outward with thumb and forefinger to zoom in on a web page, photo, map or document.

Pinch together with thumb and forefinger to zoom back out on a web page, photo, map or document.

Swiping outward with thumb and forefinger enables you to zoom in on an item to a greater degree than when double-tapping with one finger.

More Gestures

- Swipe left or right with four or five fingers to move between open apps.

- Drag with two or three fingers to move a web page, photo, map or document.

- Swipe down on any free area on the Home screen to access the Spotlight Search box.

- Swipe left or right with one finger to move between full-size photos in the Photos app.

- Tap once on a photo thumbnail with one finger to enlarge it to full screen within the Photos app.

- Drag down from the top right-hand corner of any screen to access the Control Center.

- Drag down at the top middle of the iPad to view current notifications in the Notification Center.

Using the Dock

The Dock is an element that has been part of the iPad since it was introduced. The Dock has two separate sections: the standard Dock area for your most frequently-used apps, and a section for recently-used apps, those open on another Apple device, and the App Library icon.

Elements of the Dock

Standard apps (by default, these are Messages, Safari, Music, Mail, Calendar, Photos, and Notes) are displayed on the left-hand side of the Dock.

Hot tip

Just above the Dock is a line of small dots. These indicate how many Home screens of content there are on the iPad. Tap on one of the dots to go to that Home screen, or swipe to the left or right to move between them. The white dot indicates the position of the current Home screen being viewed.

Dynamic items that change each time a new app is opened, or certain apps opened on another Apple device using iPadOS, iOS or macOS are displayed on the right-hand side (and also the App Library icon at the far right-hand side).

Don't forget

The functionality of open apps on other Apple devices is known as **Handoff** and can be turned **On** or **Off** in **Settings** > **General** > **AirPlay & Handoff**.

If a compatible app is open on another Apple device – e.g. an iPhone – this label appears in the right-hand corner. Tap on the app to open the same item as is displaying on the other

Apple device. Apps that operate in this way are those linked through iCloud, and include the web browser Safari, Mail, Messages, Reminders, Calendar, Contacts, and Notes. The icon on the far right-hand side of the Dock is for the App Library; see pages 36-37 for details.

Adding and removing Dock items

Default items on the Dock can be removed and other apps added, as required. To do this:

 Press and hold on an item on the Dock until all items start to wobble, and drag it onto the main area of the Home screen

 Repeat the process for an app on the Home screen to drag it onto the Dock

Accessing the Dock

The Dock can also be accessed from any app, not just from the Home screen. To do this:

 From within any app, use a short swipe up from the bottom of the screen to access the Dock

Up to 14 apps can be added to the left-hand side of the Dock. However, this reduces the size at which the apps' icons appear. There are only ever four items on the right-hand side of the Dock, and this changes each time a new app is opened or accessed (unless it is already in the main area of the Dock).

31

Press the **Home** button once to return to the Home screen (displaying the Dock) from any app, or swipe up from the bottom of the screen if your iPad does not have a **Home** button.

Widgets on the Home Screen

The iPad Home screen contains icons for the apps that can be accessed, and also widgets containing items of useful information, which are located at the top of the Home screen.

By default, these widgets are, from left to right: the **Clock** widget, the **Notes** widget, the **Calendar** widget, and two stacks of widgets (several widgets together), initially displaying the **News** widget and the **Weather** widget.

Beware

Widgets cannot be placed within another widget: if they are moved over another widget, it will move aside to accommodate them.

Press and hold anywhere on the Home screen to access the editing controls for widgets.

Don't forget

If all widgets are removed from the Home screen (see the Don't forget tip on the next page), the apps on the Home screen will be rearranged to take up the available space. If widgets are then reinstated, they will take up their original position on the Home screen.

To use widgets on the Home screen:

1   Tap once on an individual widget to open the full version of the app

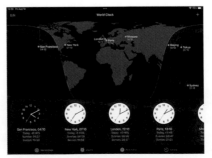

2 For stacks, swipe up or down to view the other widgets in a stack

3 Tap once on the active widget in a stack to open the full version of the app

4 Press and hold a widget to access its own menu options

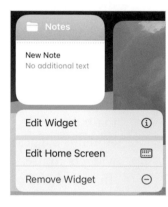

33

Moving widgets

Widgets on the Home screen can be moved around so that you can order the panel exactly how you want. To do this:

1 Press and hold on a widget on the Home screen until the controls appear

2 Drag the widget into a new position. Widgets remain at their selected sizes, and other widgets will be reordered to accommodate the moved widget accordingly

...cont'd

Adding Home screen widgets

Widgets on the Home screen can be customized to display different apps and at different sizes. To do this:

Widgets and stacks can also be edited from the Home screen. For stacks, press and hold on a stack and tap once on the **Edit Stack** button.

Edit Stack	🗄
Edit Home Screen	⌨
Remove Stack	⊖

For widgets, press and hold on a widget and tap once on the **Edit Widget** button, if this is available.

Edit Widget	ⓘ
Edit Home Screen	⌨
Remove Widget	⊖

1 Press and hold on the Home screen widgets until they start to wobble (or, if they have all been removed, press and hold anywhere on the Home screen). Tap once the **+** button in the top left-hand corner

2 The Widgets Library is displayed. The main panel contains suggested widgets to use. The left-hand sidebar contains a full list of available widgets. The Search box at the top of the window can be used to search for specific widgets

3 Tap once on a widget to view options for adding it to the Home screen. Swipe from right to left, or tap on the dots toward the bottom of the window, to access the different sizes and formats at which the widget can be used

4 Tap once on the **Add Widget** button. The widget is added to the Home screen, at the size selected in Step 3

Today View Panel

The Today View panel contains similar widgets to the Home screen, but they are not displayed on the Home screen. To use the Today View panel:

 Swipe from left to right on the left hand edge of the Home screen to access the Today View panel, which contains Today View widgets

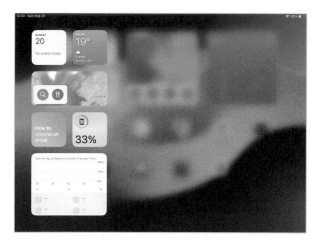

 Press and hold anywhere within the Today View panel to access its editing controls. Tap once on the **+** button to add more widgets

Swipe up on the Today View panel to see all of the widgets currently in it. Tap once on the **Edit** button at the bottom of the Today View panel to access the editing controls for the widgets.

Tap once on the **−** button to remove a widget

Using the App Library

By default, apps on iPads with iPadOS have always appeared on separate Home screens, once there are too many for one Home screen. While this is still the case, iPadOS 17 can also display all apps on the device, organized into separate categories and folders. This is known as the App Library. To use the App Library to work with and manage the apps on your iPad:

1 Tap once on the App Library icon on the Dock

2 Apps in the App Library are automatically organized into appropriate folders. Tap once on an app in a folder to open it

Beware

The order of the folders in the App Library cannot be changed; i.e. you cannot move them around within the App Library.

3 Tap once on the corner of a folder to open it and view all of the apps within it

4 Press and hold anywhere on the App Library page to access the control buttons. Tap once on this button to delete an app from your iPad

Viewing apps
To view all of the apps in the App Library:

1 Swipe downward anywhere within the App Library

2 All of the available apps are listed alphabetically

3 Swipe up and down to view all available apps, or tap on the alphabetic sidebar to move to that section

4 Use the Search box at the top of the App Library window to search for specific apps. As you type, matching apps will appear below the Search box

Using the Control Center

The Control Center is a panel containing commonly-used options within the **Settings** app, and is an excellent option for when you do not want to have to go into Settings.

Accessing the Control Center
The Control Center can be accessed from any screen within iPadOS 17, and it can also be accessed from the Lock screen.

1 Swipe down from the top right-hand corner of the Home screen, from any app, or from the Lock screen, to access the Control Center panel

Control Center functionality
The Control Center contains items that have differing formats and functionality. To access these:

1 Press on the folder of four icons to access **Airplane Mode**, **AirDrop**, **Wi-Fi** and **Bluetooth** options

Don't forget

AirDrop is the functionality for sharing items wirelessly between compatible devices. Tap once on the **AirDrop** button in the Control Center and specify whether you want to share with **Contacts Only** or **Everyone**. Once AirDrop is set up, you can use the **Share** button in compatible apps to share items such as photos with any other AirDrop users in the vicinity.

2 Press on the **Music** button to expand the options for music controls, including playing or pausing items and changing the volume. Tap once on this icon to send music from your iPad to other compatible devices, such as AirPod earphones or HomePods (Apple's wireless speakers)

3 Tap once on individual buttons to turn items **On** or **Off** (they change color depending on their state)

4 Drag on these items to increase or decrease the screen brightness and the volume

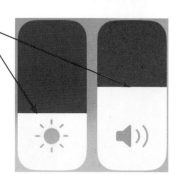

When **Airplane Mode** is activated in the second Step 1 on the previous page, network and wireless connectivity on the iPad is disabled. However, it can still be used for functions such as playing music or reading books, as long as they have been downloaded to the iPad.

39

Press on the **Brightness** and **Volume** buttons to access panels that allow greater precision by dragging on their respective bars.

The Control Center also has a **Screen Mirroring** option, for displaying what is on the iPad on a compatible High-Definition TV.

...cont'd

Control Center options
Items in the Control Center can be accessed as follows:

- Tap once on this button to turn **Airplane Mode** On or Off.

- Tap once on this button to activate **AirDrop** for sharing items with other AirDrop users.

- Tap once on this button to turn **Wi-Fi** On or Off.

- Tap once on this button to turn **Bluetooth** On or Off.

- Tap once on this button to **Lock** or **Unlock** screen rotation. If it is locked, the screen will not change when you change the orientation of your iPad.

- Tap once on this button to **Mute** all sounds.

- Tap once on this button to turn **Focus** mode On or Off.

- Tap once on this button to access the **Notes** app. Press on the button to access options for creating new notes or checklists.

- Tap once on this button to open the **Camera** app. Press on the button to access options for taking a selfie (a self-portrait) or recording a video.

...cont'd

Customizing the Control Center

Items in the Control Center can be customized – i.e. items can be added or removed. To do this:

1 Tap once on the **Settings** app

2 Tap once on the **Control Center** tab

3 Items currently in the Control Center are shown at the top of the window; those that can be added are below them. Tap once on a red icon to remove an existing item, or tap once on a green icon to add new items to the Control Center

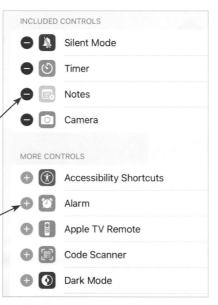

4 Items that are added in Step 3 are included in the Control Center, and can be accessed from here

Dark Mode, for changing the screen background and text color, can also be added to the Control Center from the list in Step 3.

Dark Mode

Customizing the Lock Screen

Customizing the Lock screen is a new feature in iPadOS 17.

Being able to customize the Lock screen has been a feature of the iPhone for over a year, since iOS 16, and it is now brought to the iPad with iPadOS 17. This enables some elements of the Lock screen to be customized in terms of changing the background, editing font and color, and adding widgets to the Lock screen so that their information can be viewed without having to unlock the iPad.

Customizing elements

To customize existing elements of the Lock screen:

The Lock screen can be activated by pressing the **On/Off** button on the side of the iPad once. It can also be accessed by swiping down from the top middle of any screen being viewed.

 Activate the Lock screen and press and hold on it to access the customization options. Swipe left or right to view the different Lock screen options and tap once on one to apply it as the current Lock screen

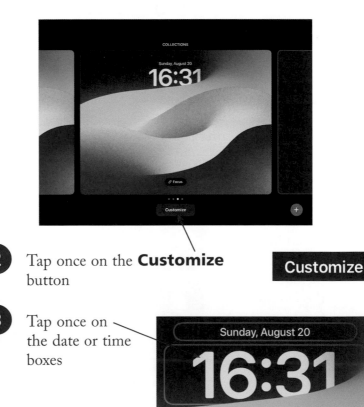

2 Tap once on the **Customize** button

Customize

The Focus function can be added to the Lock screen by tapping once on the **Focus** button in Step 1. See pages 56-57 for more details about using the Focus function.

3 Tap once on the date or time boxes

Sunday, August 20

16:31

🔗 **Focus**

Select new fonts and colors for the date and time boxes, as required

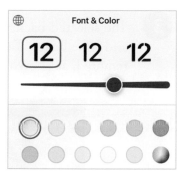

 Tap once on the **Done** button in the top right-hand corner of the customization screen to apply any changes made in Step 4

Changing the background

To change the background of the Lock screen:

 Activate the customization options as shown in Step 1 on the previous page and tap once on this button

 The available background options are displayed. Swipe up and down to view more backgrounds. Tap once on a background to select it

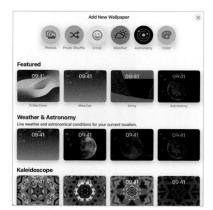

Don't forget

Options for changing the Lock screen background can also be accessed from the initial customization screen; see page 44.

Hot tip

Tap once on the **Photos** option on the top toolbar in Step 2 to see photos from your own photo library that can be used as the Lock screen background.

...cont'd

 3 The selected background is shown with the date and time boxes. Tap once on these to edit them, if required, as shown on page 42

4 Tap once on the **Add** button to apply the selected Lock screen background

5 Tap once on the **Set as Wallpaper Pair** button to apply the background to the Lock screen and the Home screen

6 The option for changing the Lock screen background can also be accessed from Step 1 on page 42 by swiping from right to left and tapping once on the **Add New** button

Tap once on the **Customize Home Screen** button in Step 5 to apply a background to the Home screen that is different from the Lock screen one.

Hot tip

...cont'd

Adding widgets

Specific widgets can also be added to the Lock screen, to give it increased functionality. To do this:

 Activate the customization options as shown in Step 1 on page 42 and tap once on the **Add Widgets** button at the left-hand side

Numerous widgets can be added to the Lock screen depending on the size of the widgets.

 Tap once on a widget in the **Add Widgets** window to add it to the Lock screen. Tap once on the – icon to remove a widget

 Once the required widgets have been selected, tap once on the **Done** button in the top right-hand corner to add the selected widgets to the Lock screen

45

Don't forget

Multitasking is most effective on iPads with larger screens.

Hot tip

The multitasking options can both still be accessed in the original way. To do this, open one app and drag up from the bottom of the screen to display the Dock. Press and hold on another app and drag it to the side of the screen to create a split view, or drag it over the first app to create a Slide Over view.

Multitasking

With iPadOS 17 there are several useful multitasking options, including **Split View**, **Slide Over** and **Full Screen**. To use the multitasking options:

1 Open the first app that you want to use

2 The **Multitasking** button at the top of the app can be used to access the multitasking options. Tap once on the button

3 The multitasking options are, from left to right: **Full Screen**, **Split View**, and **Slide Over**. Tap once on each option to apply it to the selected app

✓ Full Screen	▪
Split View	⊞
Slide Over	◱
Close	×

Using Split View

Split View enables two apps to be used side by side, independently of each other. For instance, you can look at a page on the web with Safari in one view, and then add notes in the Notes app in the other view. To use Split View:

1 Open the first app that you want to use and tap once on the **Multitasking** button at the top of the window, as shown in Step 1 above

2 Tap once on the **Split View** option

Split View	⊞

3 The app is minimized to the left-hand side of the screen and the Home screen is displayed

The **Split View** button at the top of the screen prompts you to select another app for Split View, at the top of the screen in Step 3.

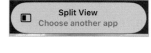

4 Tap once on an app on the Home screen, or on the Dock, to activate it as the other app in Split View

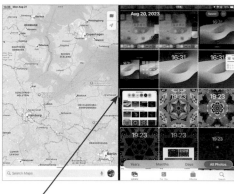

Tap once on the **Multitasking** button in either of the Split View windows and tap once on the **Full Screen** option to make that window full screen, and close Split View.

5 The two apps are displayed side by side. Initially, the apps in Split View take up 50% of the screen each and can be used independently of each other. Drag on the middle button to change the proportions of the two Split View panels

6 Press and hold on the middle button and drag it away from the right-hand (or left-hand) edge of the screen to close one of the Split View apps

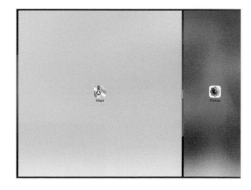

...cont'd

Using Slide Over view

Slide Over view is similar to Split View, except the second app appears as a floating panel over the initial one. Also, the Slide Over panel can contain multiple apps. To use Slide Over view for multitasking:

 Open the first app that you want to use and tap once on the **Multitasking** button at the top of the window, as shown on page 46

 Tap once on the **Slide Over** view option

| Slide Over | ▢ |

 The app is minimized to the right-hand side of the screen and the Home screen is displayed

Don't forget

The **Slide Over** button at the top of the screen prompts you to select another app for **Slide Over**, once it has been selected in Step 2.

Tap once on an app on the Home screen, or on the Dock, to activate it in Slide Over view

5 Press and hold on the button at the top of the Slide Over panel to drag it to either side of the screen (or swipe on the button, from right to left)

Hot tip

Multiple apps can be added to the panel in Slide Over view, by dragging up from the bottom of the screen to display the Dock, and then dragging more apps into the Slide Over panel. Press on the dark bar at the bottom of the app and swipe to the right or left to reveal the next available apps in Slide Over view.

6 The two apps can be used independently of each other; e.g. move through different web pages in Safari or search locations in Maps

Shelf and New Windows

Another multitasking option is the **Shelf**, which can be thought of as a temporary storage location within compatible apps so that you can keep one item open while you are looking at something else. The apps that support this feature are Notes, Safari and Mail. The Shelf also enables new windows to be opened and used for these apps. To use the **Shelf**:

 Open one of the apps that supports the **Shelf** – e.g. the Notes app

 Press and hold on a note in the left-hand sidebar until its menu appears. Tap once on the **Open in New Window** button

Hot tip

Tap once on the **Close** button in the top left-hand corner of the window in Step 3 to close the window without adding it to the Shelf.

3 The note opens in its own window, floating over the main Notes window

4 Tap once anywhere on the main Notes window. The note in the new window is now placed on the **Shelf**, displayed at the bottom of the window. Tap once on an item on the **Shelf** to make it the active one

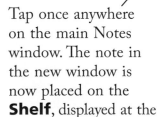

5 Tap once on the **Multitasking** button at the top of the main Notes window to access items in the **Shelf** at the bottom of the screen

6 Tap once on an item on the **Shelf** to make it the active one. Tap once on the **New Window** button to open a new window for the app

Hot tip

To remove items from the **Shelf**, press and hold on them and swipe them to the top of the screen.

51

Using the Shelf in Safari

To use new windows and the **Shelf** in Safari:

1 Open a web page in Safari, then swipe up from the bottom of the screen to access the Dock, and tap once on the Safari icon

2 The currently-open page is displayed on the **Shelf**. Tap once on the **New Window** button to open a new window for Safari

Don't forget

The **Shelf** can also be accessed in Notes and Mail in the same way as for Safari; i.e. open the app and then access the same app again from the Dock, to activate the Shelf and the **New Window** button.

Using the Shelf in Mail

Using the **Shelf** in Mail is similar to using it in Notes: press and hold on an email in your Inbox in Mail and tap on the **Open in New Window** button in the same way as in Step 2 on the previous page. Access the email in the same way as for a note on the previous page, and access the **Shelf** in the same way too.

App Switcher Window

The **App Switcher** feature in iPadOS 17 performs a number of shortcuts and useful tasks:

● It shows open apps and enables you to move between these and access them by tapping once on the required item.

● It enables apps to be closed (see the next page).

Accessing App Switcher

The App Switcher window can be accessed from any screen on your iPad, as follows:

Don't forget

If your iPad does not have a **Home** button, use the option in Step 2 to access the App Switcher and look at the screen while you're swiping up, to activate Face ID.

 Double-click on the **Home** button, or

Hot tip

Swipe up from the bottom of the screen slightly further than the middle of the screen to return to the Home screen, rather than the App Switcher.

2 Swipe up from the bottom of any screen. This should be a long swipe, up to the middle of the screen at least. A short swipe will bring up the Dock at the bottom of the screen, rather than the App Switcher

3 Tap once on an app in the App Switcher to make it the active one

Closing apps

The iPad deals with open apps very efficiently. They rarely interact with other apps, which increases security and also means that they can be open in the background, without using up a significant amount of processing power, in a state of semi hibernation until they are needed. Because of this, it is not essential to close apps when you move to something else. However, you may want to close apps if you feel you have too many open or if one stops working. To do this:

1 Access the App Switcher window. The currently-open apps are displayed

2 Press and hold on an app and swipe it to the top of the screen to close it. This does not remove it from the iPad, and it can be opened again in the usual way

3 The app is removed from its position in the App Switcher window and the other apps move to fill the space

Keeping Notified

Although the **Notification Center** feature is not an app in its own right, it can be used to display information from a variety of apps. The notifications appear as a list of all items you want to be reminded about or made aware of. Notifications are set up within the Settings app. To do this:

1 Tap once on the **Settings** app

2 Tap once on the **Notifications** tab

3 In the **Notification Style** section, tap once on an item to determine how it operates when it displays a notification

4 Drag the **Allow Notifications** button **On** to allow notifications to be displayed for this item

5 Make selections for where and how you want the notification to appear. This includes the Lock screen, the Notification Center, and as an onscreen banner

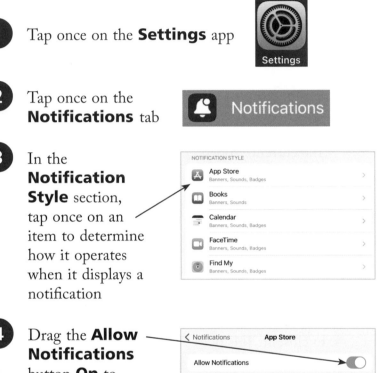

Don't forget

Use the Scheduled Summary (tap once on the **Scheduled Summary** button in the main **Notifications** window) to specify settings for grouping notifications and displaying them at a specific time.

6 Drag the **Time Sensitive Notifications** button **On** to enable notifications to be displayed as soon as they become active, if they are time-specific; e.g. for a calendar event at a specific time

ALWAYS DELIVER IMMEDIATELY

🕐   **Time Sensitive Notifications**

Viewing notifications

Once the Notifications settings have been selected, they can be used to keep up-to-date with all of your important appointments and reminders via the Notification Center. To view the Notification Center:

1 Drag down from the top of any screen to view the Notification Center. This displays items that have been selected, as shown on the previous page, at the bottom of the screen. This is also the case if the Lock screen is active

Reminders
New Reminder   now

2 Tap once on an item to open it in its own app

Today

Morning

○   **Water plants**
Reminders – 09:40

Focus

Another option for managing your notifications is the **Focus** function, which can be used to control when you are notified about certain items. The Focus function can be used to limit notifications when you are performing certain actions (e.g. reading or relaxing), and it can also specify certain people and apps that are allowed to contact you and send notifications. The Focus function can be set up within the Settings app, and also accessed from the Control Center. To do this:

The Focus function also contains the **Do Not Disturb** feature. To set this up, tap once on the **Do Not Disturb** button in Step 3 and select the required options and times for when you want **Do Not Disturb** to operate.

Different focuses can be set for specific activities, and the settings for the focus can be applied according to the required activity.

1 Tap once on the **Settings** app

2 Tap once on the **Focus** tab

3 Tap once on the **+** button in the top right-hand corner

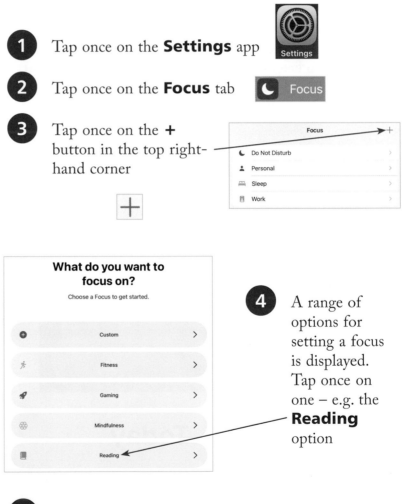

4 A range of options for setting a focus is displayed. Tap once on one – e.g. the **Reading** option

5 Tap once on the **Customize Focus** button

...cont'd

6 Tap once on the **Choose People** button, to add someone from whom notifications can still appear. Tap once on the **Choose Apps** button to specify certain apps that can be active during the focus period

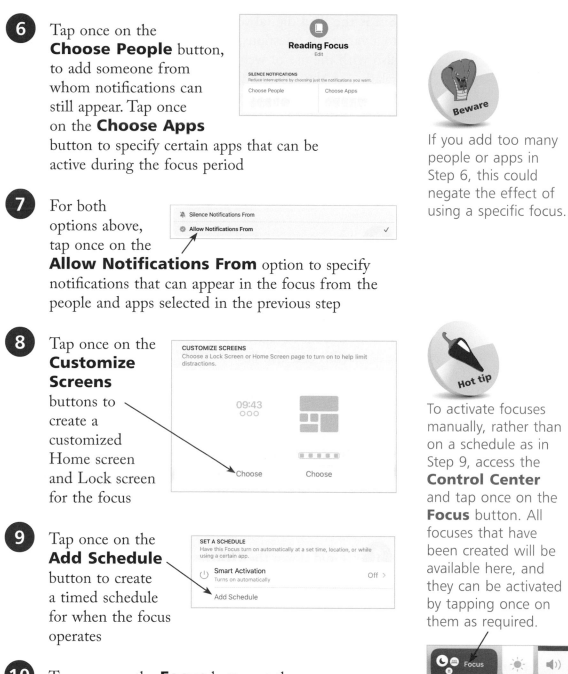

Reading Focus
Edit

SILENCE NOTIFICATIONS
Reduce interruptions by choosing just the notifications you want.

Choose People   Choose Apps

Beware

If you add too many people or apps in Step 6, this could negate the effect of using a specific focus.

7 For both options above, tap once on the **Allow Notifications From** option to specify notifications that can appear in the focus from the people and apps selected in the previous step

Silence Notifications From
Allow Notifications From   ✓

8 Tap once on the **Customize Screens** buttons to create a customized Home screen and Lock screen for the focus

CUSTOMIZE SCREENS
Choose a Lock Screen or Home Screen page to turn on to help limit distractions.

09:43
OOO

Choose   Choose

Hot tip

To activate focuses manually, rather than on a schedule as in Step 9, access the **Control Center** and tap once on the **Focus** button. All focuses that have been created will be available here, and they can be activated by tapping once on them as required.

9 Tap once on the **Add Schedule** button to create a timed schedule for when the focus operates

SET A SCHEDULE
Have this Focus turn on automatically at a set time, location, or while using a certain app.

Smart Activation
Turns on automatically   Off >

Add Schedule

10 Tap once on the **Focus** button at the top of the screen to complete the focus

< Focus

57

Finding Things with Siri

Siri is the iPad digital voice assistant that provides answers to a variety of questions, by looking within your iPad and also with the use of web services. You can ask Siri questions relating to the apps on your iPad, and also general questions such as weather conditions around the world, or sports results. Initially, Siri can be set up within the Settings app.

Hot tip

Siri can be used to open any of the built-in iPad apps, simply by saying, for example, "Open Photos".

1 Tap once on the **Siri & Search** option

 Siri & Search

2 Tap once on the options to select a language, set voice feedback, and allow access to your details (Siri can also be set up when you first start to use your iPad)

Siri & Search	
ASK SIRI	
Listen for	"Siri" or "Hey Siri" >
Press Home for Siri	⬤
Allow Siri When Locked	⬤
Language	English (United States) >
Siri Voice	American (Voice 2) >

Hot tip

Tap once on the **Listen for** option in the first Step 2, and tap once on the **"Siri" or "Hey Siri"** option to activate Siri just by saying either of these phrases without having to press the **Home** button.

Questioning Siri

Once you have set up Siri, you can start putting it to work with your queries. To do this:

1 Hold down the **Home** button until the Siri window appears

📅 Calendar

THURSDAY, AUG 24

| Green | all-day |

| Tennis match | 18:00 23:00 |

Next

Don't forget

For iPads that do not have a **Home** button, hold down the **On/ Off** button to access Siri.

2 To find something within your iPad apps, make a request such as "Show me my calendar"

Siri can also find information from across the web and related web services.

1 Siri can provide sports results for certain sports in certain countries, such as in response to the request "Show Red Sox latest details"

Siri can be used with a range of Apple and specific third-party apps. For instance, you can ask it to find specific photos in the Photos app, send a message to someone with the Messages app, and even book restaurants and taxis with compatible apps.

2 Global weather reports are another of Siri's strong points, and it can provide forecasts in response to the request "Show me the hourly weather in San Francisco"

3 Siri can also display a range of information in relation to nearby establishments such as restaurants, movie theaters and museums. Try asking, "Show me nearby Italian restaurants"

Spotlight Search

Items can also be searched for using the Spotlight Search option. To do this:

 1 Swipe downward on the Home screen to access the Spotlight **Search** box

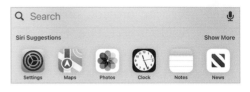

 2 Enter a keyword or phrase in the Search box at the top of the window

Spotlight Search can also be used to search for local businesses and services, such as local restaurants and movie theaters, either by using specific names or by asking it to show a certain type of restaurant nearby.

3 Swipe up the panel to view all search results

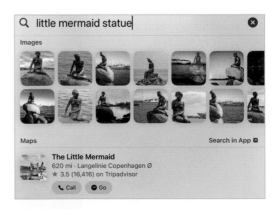

3 iCloud

This chapter shows how to use the online iCloud services for storing and sharing content.

Living in the iCloud

iCloud is the Apple online service that performs a number of valuable functions:

- It makes your content available across multiple devices. The content is stored in iCloud and then pushed out to other iCloud-enabled devices, including the iPhone and other Mac or Windows computers.

- It enables online access to your content via the iCloud website, with your Apple ID details (**www.icloud.com**). This includes your iCloud email, Contacts, Calendar, Notes, and Reminders.

- It can back up the content of your iPad.

Once you have registered for and set up iCloud, it works automatically so you do not have to worry about anything. You can activate iCloud when you first set up your iPad, or:

Another useful iCloud function is iCloud Keychain (**Settings > Apple ID, iCloud, Media & Purchases > iCloud > Passwords and Keychain**). This can keep all of your passwords and bank card information up-to-date across multiple devices and remember this when you use them on websites. The information is encrypted and controlled through your Apple ID.

1 Tap once on the **Settings** app

2 At the top of the Settings panel, tap once on the **Sign in to your iPad** option

Settings

Q Search

Sign in to your iPad
Set up iCloud, the App Store, and more.

3 If you already have an Apple ID, enter your details and tap once on the **Sign in Manually** option

Apple ID

Choose the method to sign in yourself or a child in your family on this device.

Use Another Apple Device
Bring another Apple device nearby to sign in quickly and easily. Available for iOS 17 and later.

Sign in Manually
Enter an email address or phone number and password then verify your identity.

Don't have an Apple ID?

4 If you do not yet have an Apple ID, tap once on the **Don't have an Apple ID?** link and follow the steps to create your Apple ID

iCloud settings

After you have set up your iCloud account, you can then apply settings for how it works. Once you have done this, you will not have to worry about it again.

1 Tap once on the **Apple ID, iCloud, Media & Purchases** tab of the Settings app

2 Tap once on the **iCloud** button

3 Tap once on these items and drag their buttons **On** for items you want to be synced with iCloud. Each item is then saved and stored in iCloud, and made available to other iCloud-enabled devices

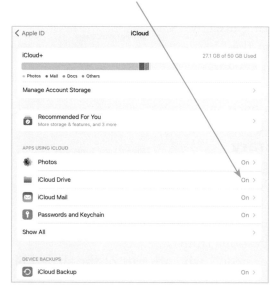

The default amount of storage for an iCloud account is 5GB, which is provided free of charge. However, it is also possible to upgrade the amount of storage, using **iCloud+**. This is a subscription service, and it can be accessed by tapping once on the **Manage Account Storage** button in Step 3, and then tapping once on the **Upgrade to iCloud+** option. In addition to being able to add extra storage options, iCloud+ also has extra features, including: **Private Relay**, which protects your browsing by ensuring that any website interactions are encrypted from your iPhone, and **Hide My Email**, which can be used to create a new, random email address each time you have to enter your email address online.

63

iCloud Shared Photo Library

iPadOS 17 also enables iCloud to create a shared photo library that can then be shared with family and friends. One of the advantages of this is that photos can be shared directly from the Camera app, when they are taken. Older photos in the Photos app can also be added to a shared library. To use a shared photo library:

Don't forget

The **Shared Library** option in Step 2 can also be accessed from **Settings** > **Photos**.

Beware

Shared albums can also be set up for the Photos app so that photos and videos can be shared with invited people, from **Settings** > **Photos** > **Shared Albums**. However, unlike the shared library, photos cannot be added directly from the Camera app, and other users cannot edit or delete photos from a shared album.

1 Access the iCloud section in the Settings app, as shown on page 63, and tap once on the **Photos** option

APPS USING ICLOUD

Photos

2 Tap once on the **Shared Library** option

LIBRARY

Shared Library
No Participants

3 In the **Shared Library** section, use these options to apply suggestions and also options for sharing directly from the Camera app

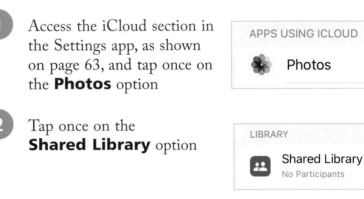

4 Tap once on the **Shared Library Suggestions** option and drag the button **On** to enable photo suggestions from other people who are part of the shared library

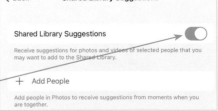

5 Tap once on the **Sharing from Camera** option in Step 3 on the previous page to select how photos

are added to the shared library when they are taken with the Camera app

6 Tap once on the **Add Participants** option in Step 3 on the previous page to select people and invite them to the shared library

7 Once someone has been invited, this is indicated in the main window. An invitation has to be accepted for someone to join the shared library

8 To add photos to the shared library from the Camera app, tap once on this icon on the top toolbar of the Camera app

9 The icon turns yellow, to indicate that the shared library feature is activated. Any photos that are taken when this icon is yellow will be added to the shared library

SHARED LIBRARY

Don't forget

Once someone has joined the shared library they have full access to add photos and videos, and also edit or delete ones that are already in the shared library.

Hot tip

Photos in the Photos app can be added to the shared library. To do this, open them at full size in the Photos app, tap once on the menu button in the top right-hand corner, and tap once on the **Move to Shared Library** option.

65

About iCloud Drive

One of the options in the iCloud section is for iCloud Drive. This can be used to store documents so that you can use them on any other Apple devices that you have, such as an iPhone or a MacBook. With iCloud Drive (and the Files app), you can start work on a document on one device and continue on another device from where you left off.

Beware

If using iCloud Drive-compatible apps (such as **Pages**, **Numbers** and **Keynote**), they should be updated to their latest versions via the App Store (see page 94).

Hot tip

Tap once on the **Files** app on the Home screen to view items that have been saved in iCloud Drive.

Files

1 Tap once on the **Apple ID, iCloud, Media & Purchases** tab of the Settings app

Nick Vandome
Apple ID, iCloud, Media & Purchases

2 Tap once on the **iCloud** button

iCloud

3 Tap once on the **iCloud Drive** button

iCloud Drive

4 Drag the **Sync this iPad** button to green to turn it **On**. This ensures that items that are stored in iCloud will be available on any other Apple devices you have, using the same Apple ID

< iCloud   iCloud Drive

iCloud Drive

Keep your files in sync with iCloud. Access and share them on all your devices and on icloud.com.
Learn more

Sync this iPad

About Family Sharing

In iPadOS 17, the Family Sharing function enables you to share items that you have downloaded from the App Store, such as music and movies, with up to five other family members, as long as they have an Apple ID account. Once this has been set up, it is also possible to share items such as family calendars and photos, and even see where family members are on a map. To set up Family Sharing:

1 Access the **iCloud** section within the Settings app, as shown on page 63

2 Tap once on the **Family Sharing** button

Family Sharing

3 Tap once on the **Continue** button

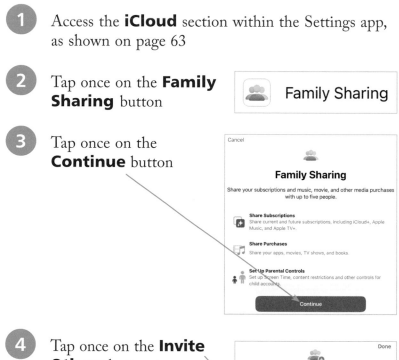

4 Tap once on the **Invite Others** button to invite family members or friends to join your Family Sharing group. This includes music, storage plans, subscriptions, App Store purchases, and location sharing for finding a lost or stolen Apple device

5 Complete the setup process by confirming your iCloud account, and specify a payment method for items that are purchased through Family Sharing

Using Family Sharing

Once you have set up Family Sharing and added family members, you can start sharing a selection of items.

Sharing subscriptions

There are a number of Apple subscription services, and if you join any of them then you can also share them via Family Sharing. This means that anyone in your Family Sharing group can take advantage of these services too, without having to pay for an additional subscription. The options include:

- **Apple Music**. If a family subscription has been taken out for Apple Music, this can be shared via Family Sharing, providing access to millions of songs.

  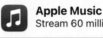
  Apple Music
  Stream 60 million songs ad-free.

- **Apple TV+**. This is Apple's subscription service for movies and TV shows. There is a wealth of original content in Apple TV+ that you cannot access elsewhere.

  Apple TV+
  New Apple Originals every month.

- **Apple Arcade**. This is a subscription gaming service, with a range of original games that can be played individually or as multiplayer games with other people.

  Apple Arcade
  Unlimited access to 200+ ad-free games.

- **Apple News+**. This an expanded version of the free news service provided by the News app.

  Apple News+
  Hundreds of magazines and leading newspapers.

- **iCloud+**. The expanded iCloud service can be made available via Family Sharing, giving access to additional levels of shared storage.

  Share iCloud+ with Family
  Give your family access to additional iCloud storage, Private Relay, Hide My Email, and other premium features at no extra charge.

  Share iCloud+

Don't forget

The regular Apple TV option can be used to rent or buy movies and TV shows. Both the regular service and Apple TV+ can be accessed from the **TV** app.

Sharing calendars

Family Sharing also generates a Family calendar that can be used by all Family Sharing members.

  Tap once on the **Calendar** app

 Tap once on this button and create a new event (see pages 134-135). Select **Family** as the calendar option to distribute the event to your Family Sharing members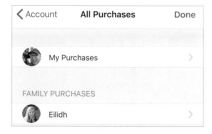

Calendar	● Family ⌄

Sharing apps, music, books and movies

Family Sharing means that all members of the group can share purchases from the iTunes Store, the App Store or the Book Store, accessed from within the Books app. This is done from the **My Purchases** section of each app.

1 Open the relevant app and access the **My Purchases** section. (For the **App Store**, tap once on the Account icon and tap once on the **Purchased** button; for the **iTunes Store**, tap once on the **Menu** > **Purchased** button on the bottom toolbar; for the **Books** app, tap once on the Account icon)

‹ Account	All Purchases	Done
	My Purchases	›
FAMILY PURCHASES		
	Eilidh	›

 For all three apps, tap once on a member under **Family Purchases** to view their purchases and download them, if required, by tapping once on this button

Don't forget

When someone in the Family Sharing group adds an event to the Family calendar, it will appear in your calendar with the appropriate tag. A red notification will also appear on the Calendar app, and it will appear in the Notification Center (if the Calendar app has been selected to appear here).

69

...cont'd

Don't
forget

The **Find My** app can also be opened directly from this icon:

Find My

Don't
forget

When the **Find My** app is opened, tap once on the **People** button to see people who have been added via Family Sharing. They must also have Location Services turned **On** (**Settings** > **Privacy & Security** > **Location Services**) so that you can locate them. Tap once on the **Devices** button to view all Apple devices that can be located with the Find My app, including your own and those of any family members who have been added.

Finding family members

Family Sharing makes it easy to keep in touch with the rest of the family and see exactly where they are. This can be done in conjunction with the Find My app. The other person must have their iPad (or other Apple device) turned on and be online. To share your location:

1 Access the **Family Sharing** section, as shown in Step 2 on page 67, tap once on the **Location Sharing** option and tap once on the **Share Location** button

Location Sharing
Not sharing with family

Share Location

2 Tap once on the **Open Find My** option

< Family

Family members you share your location with can also see the location of your devices in Find My. This way if your device is lost or stolen, you can ask them to help you locate it. Learn more...

SHARE YOUR LOCATION WITH

No family member is sharing their location with you.

Automatically Share Location

Automatically share your location with any new family members that join later.

Open Find My

3 The **Find My** app is opened. Select the **People** option and tap once on the **Start Sharing Location**

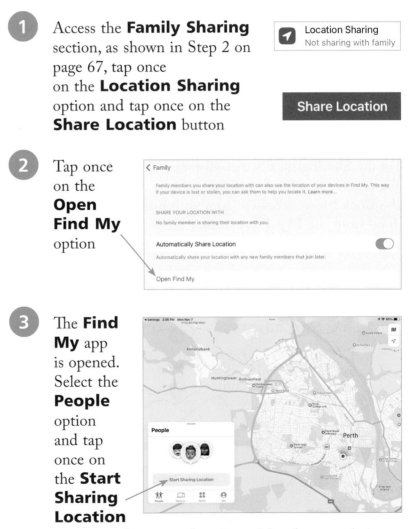

option to share your location with other people in your Family Sharing group

4 Keyboard and Apple Pencil

The iPad has a virtual keyboard and can also be used with an external one. This chapter shows how to manage the keyboard, and the Apple Pencil, for entering text.

In addition to the iPad virtual keyboard, it is also possible to use external keyboards with the iPad – see page 15 for details.

It's Virtually a Keyboard

By default, the keyboard on the iPad is a virtual one; i.e. it appears on the touchscreen whenever text or numbered input is required. This can be for a variety of reasons:

- Entering text with a word processing app, email, or an organization app such as Notes.

- Entering a web address into a web browser such as the Safari app.

- Entering information into a form.

- Entering a password.

Viewing the keyboard

When you attempt one of the items above, the keyboard appears so that you can enter any text or numbers:

Around the keyboard

To access the various keyboard controls:

1 Tap once on the **Shift** button to create a **Cap** (capital) text letter

2 Double-tap on the **Shift** button to enable **Caps Lock**

3 Tap once on this button to back-delete an item

To return from Caps Lock, tap again on the **Shift/Caps** button.

Additional buttons

In iPadOS 17, letters, numbers and symbols can all be accessed from a single keyboard. To do this:

1 Swipe down on one of the keys on the top line of the keyboard to enter the equivalent number, rather than a letter

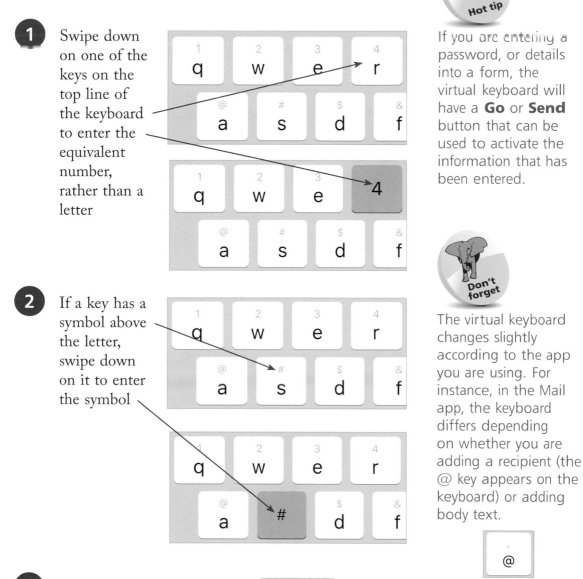

2 If a key has a symbol above the letter, swipe down on it to enter the symbol

3 Tap once on this button to hide the keyboard

Hot tip

If you are entering a password, or details into a form, the virtual keyboard will have a **Go** or **Send** button that can be used to activate the information that has been entered.

Don't forget

The virtual keyboard changes slightly according to the app you are using. For instance, in the Mail app, the keyboard differs depending on whether you are adding a recipient (the @ key appears on the keyboard) or adding body text.

73

The keyboard can also be split by swiping outward on both sides, with one finger on each side. Reverse the process to merge it again.

Floating mode for the keyboard can also be activated by pinching inward on the keyboard with two fingers. Swipe outward with two fingers to return it to its default state.

The floating keyboard can also be returned to its default state by dragging it to the bottom of the window.

Moving the Keyboard

By default, the virtual keyboard appears as a single unit along the bottom of the screen. However, it is possible to undock the keyboard and also split it to appear on either side of the screen. To do this:

1 Press and hold this button on the keyboard

2 Tap once on the **Undock** button

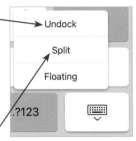

3 The keyboard is undocked from the bottom of the screen and can be moved around the screen by pressing and holding on the button in Step 1

4 Tap once on the **Split** button in Step 2 to split the keyboard to the left and right sides of the screen

5 Tap once on the **Floating** button in Step 2 to create a minimized version of the keyboard, which can be dragged around the screen using the bar at the bottom

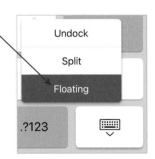

6 To redock the keyboard, press and hold on the button in Step 1 and tap once on the required command

Entering Text

Once you have applied the keyboard settings that you require, you can start entering text. To do this:

1 Tap once on the text entry area to activate the keyboard. Start typing with the keyboard. Text will appear at the point where you tapped on the screen, indicated by the flashing cursor

2 If **Predictive** (see page 79) is **Off**, as you type, Auto-Correction comes up with suggestions. Tap once on the spacebar to accept the suggestion, or tap once on the cross next to it to reject it

> Remem
> Remember ✕

3 Any misspelled words appear underlined in red

> Remember to go to the supermarkt |

4 Tap once on this button to hide the keyboard

If **Predictive** is **On**, the suggested word will appear above the keyboard on the QuickType bar (see page 79).

If you keep typing as normal, the Auto-Correction suggestion will disappear when you finish the word.

The virtual keyboard can be used for slide typing, whereby text is added by swiping over the letters on the keyboard. This can be set up in **Settings > General > Keyboard** by turning **Slide on Floating Keyboard to Type** to **On**.

Editing Text

Once text has been entered it can be selected, copied, cut and pasted. Depending on the app being used, text can also be formatted, such as with a word processing app.

Managing text

To work with text in a document you have created:

 1 To change the insertion point in a document, press on the cursor to pick it up

Moving the cursor.|

2 Drag the cursor to move the insertion point

Moving |the cursor.

 3 Tap once at the insertion point to access the menu buttons

| Paste | Select | Select All | Insert Drawing | AutoFill | Add Link | Format |

Working with |text on the iPad

4 Double-tap on a word to select it. Tap once on one of the menu buttons, as required

| Cut | Copy | Paste | Replace... | AutoFill | Add Link | Format | Find Selection | > |

Working with text on the iPad|

 5 Use the Shortcuts bar on the keyboard to, from left to right: cut the selection; copy the selection; or paste an item

Selecting text

Text can be selected using a range of methods:

1 Double-tap on a word to select it

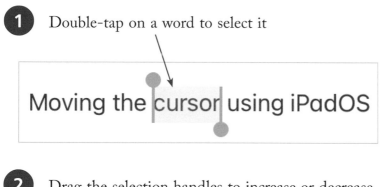

Moving the cursor using iPadOS

2 Drag the selection handles to increase or decrease the selection. This is a good way to select certain text within a sentence or within a paragraph. (Text can also be selected by dragging on the selected word, rather than using the selection handles)

Moving the cursor using iPadOS

3 Triple-tap on a word to select the whole of its related paragraph

Cut	Copy	Paste	AutoFill	Add Link	Format	Find Selection	Translate	Share...

The onscreen keyboard is always there for responding to emails or taking notes. You can also use a physical keyboard like Apple's Magic Keyboard if you want to. And with iPadOS, there are always more ways to use both.

Don't forget

Once text has been selected, there are a range of gestures that can be used to copy and paste it, and also undo the previous action. To copy selected text: pinch inward over the text with thumb and two fingers. To paste text: swipe outward with thumb and two fingers, in a dropping motion. To undo the previous action: swipe from right to left with three fingers.

Keyboard Settings

Settings for the keyboard can be determined in the **General** section of the Settings app. To do this:

The **Auto-Correction** function works as you type a word, so it may change a number of times, depending on the length of the word you are typing.

 Select **Settings > General** and tap once on the **Keyboard** option

Keyboard

Auto-Capitalization	⬤
Auto-Correction	⬤
Check Spelling	⬤
Enable Caps Lock	⬤
Shortcuts	⬤

 Drag the **Auto-Capitalization** button **On** to ensure letters will automatically be capitalized at the beginning of a sentence

 Drag the **Auto-Correction** button **On** to ensure suggestions for words will appear as you type

 Drag the **Check Spelling** button **On** to spell-check words as you type

 Drag the **Enable Caps Lock** button **On** to enable this function to be performed

 Drag the **"."** **Shortcut** button (further down the Keyboard settings screen) **On** to enable the functionality for adding a period/full stop with a double tap of the spacebar

For more information about Text Replacement, see page 81.

7 Tap once on the **Keyboards** option to access options for adding different keyboards

Keyboards
Text Replacement

8 Tap once on the **Text Replacement** option to view existing text shortcuts and also to create new ones

78

Using Predictive Text

Predictive text tries to guess what you are typing, and also predicts the next word following the one you have just typed. It was developed primarily for text messaging, and it is included on the iPad with iPadOS 17. To use it:

1 Tap once on the **General** tab in the Settings app

2 Tap once on the **Keyboard** option

3 Drag the **Predictive** button **On**

4 When **Predictive** is activated, the QuickType bar is displayed above the keyboard. Initially, this has a suggestion for the first word to include. Tap on a word, or start typing

5 As you type, suggestions appear. Tap on one to accept it. Tap on the word within quotation marks to accept exactly what you have typed, or tap on another option

6 After you have typed a word, a suggestion for the next word appears. This can be selected by tapping on it, or ignored

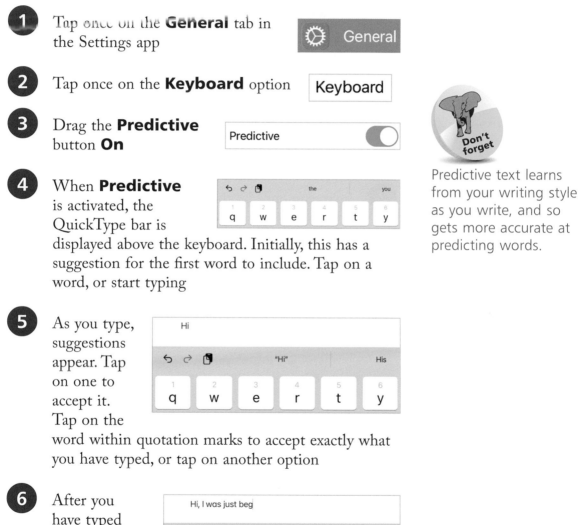

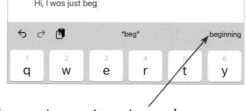

Predictive text learns from your writing style as you write, and so gets more accurate at predicting words.

Keyboard Shortcuts

There are two types of shortcuts that can be used on the iPad keyboard:

● Shortcuts using keys on the keyboard

● Shortcuts created with text abbreviations

Shortcuts with keys

Here are some examples of shortcuts that can be created with keys on the keyboard:

1 Double-tap on the spacebar to add a full stop/period and a space at the end of a sentence

○ The end. |

2 Swipe up once on the comma (or press and hold) to insert an apostrophe

3 Swipe up once on the full stop/period to insert quotation marks

4 Press and hold on appropriate letters to access accented versions for different languages

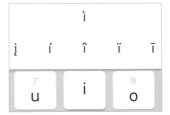

Text abbreviations

To create shortcuts with text abbreviations:

1 Tap once on the **Keyboard** option in the **General** section of the Settings app

> **Keyboard**

2 Tap once on the **Text Replacement** option

> Text Replacement

3 Tap once on this button to add a new shortcut +

4 Enter the phrase you want to be made into a shortcut

> Phrase   My name is Nick

5 Enter the abbreviation you want to use as a shortcut for the phrase

> Shortcut   mnn|

6 Tap once on the **Save** button

> Save

7 The shortcut is displayed here

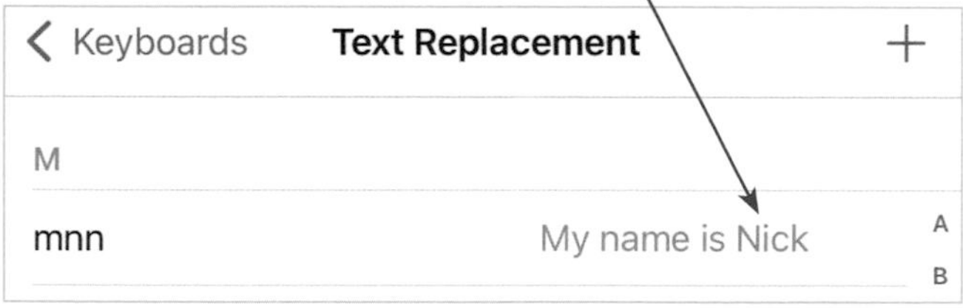

> ⟨ Keyboards   **Text Replacement**   +
>
> M
>
> mnn   My name is Nick   A
>   B

8 Use the Search box or the alphabetical bar at the right-hand side to search for other shortcuts that have been created

Don't forget

A shortcut does not need to have the equivalent number of letters as words in a phrase. A 10-word phrase could have a two-letter shortcut.

Hot tip

To use a shortcut, enter the abbreviation. As you type, the phrase appears underneath the abbreviation. Tap once on the spacebar to add the phrase, or tap once on the cross to reject it. To delete a shortcut, in the **Text Replacement** section in Step 7, swipe on it from right to left and tap once on the **Delete** button.

At the time of printing, the latest version of the Apple Pencil is the Apple Pencil 2nd generation, although this is only compatible with a more limited range of newer iPads. In October 2023, Apple announced a USB-C version of the Apple Pencil, for this type of connector.

The Scribble option is activated in **Settings > Apple Pencil** by dragging the **Scribble** button **On**.

Using the Apple Pencil

The Apple Pencil is an excellent option for getting creative with drawing apps and it is also very effective in a range of text tasks, including converting handwriting, deleting text and selecting text.

Scribble

The Apple Pencil can be used to create handwritten text in compatible apps. In some cases, this can then be converted automatically into typed text. This works in any text field, and the text can then be edited in several ways. This is known as Scribble. To use Scribble with the Apple Pencil:

 In a text box, or a Search box, use the Apple Pencil to enter handwritten text

 When you finish writing a word, it will be converted to typed text, with relevant options displayed, depending on the text box in which it is entered

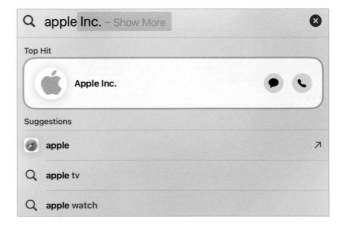

Deleting text

Text in a text field (including a web browser address bar) can be deleted using the Apple Pencil. This can be done if it is entered as handwriting and then converted to text, or entered directly from the keyboard.

 Enter text into a text box or web browser

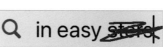

 If there is a mistake in a word, scribble over it with the Apple Pencil

 The word is deleted

Selecting text

The Apple Pencil can also be used to select text in a text field, after which editing options can be applied to it.

1 Circle the required text item with the Apple Pencil. This can be a single word, or several

2 The circled text is selected and available editing options are displayed

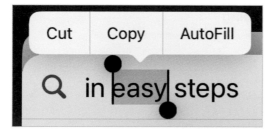

Hot tip

Press and hold with the Apple Pencil in any text field to create a space to write or type another word.

Hot tip

Draw a line between letters to create a space between them, or draw a line in the space between two words to remove the space and join the words together.

Beware

Voice typing is not an exact science, and you may find that some strange examples appear. The best results are created if you speak as clearly as possible and reasonably slowly.

Hot tip

The first time that you tap on the **Microphone** button, you may be prompted to select the **Enable Dictation** button too. This can also be done within **Settings** > **General** > **Keyboard** > **Enable Dictation**.

Don't forget

There are other voice-typing apps available from the App Store. Two to try are Dragon Anywhere and Dictation - Speech to text.

Voice Typing

On the keyboard there is also a voice-typing option, which enables you to enter text by speaking into a microphone, rather than typing on the keyboard. This is **On** by default.

Using voice typing

Voice typing can be used with any app with a text-input function. To do this:

 Tap once on this button on the keyboard to activate the voice-typing microphone. Speak into the microphone to record text

 As the voice-typing function is processing the recording, this screen appears

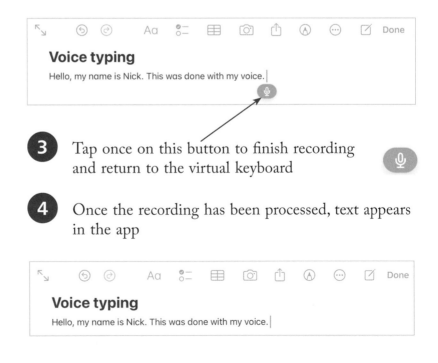

Tap once on this button to finish recording and return to the virtual keyboard

Once the recording has been processed, text appears in the app

5 Knowing your Apps

Apps keep the iPad engine running. This chapter details the built-in ones and shows how to review and download more through the App Store.

Don't forget

You need an active internet connection to download apps from the App Store.

Hot tip

Within a number of apps there is a **Share** button that can be used to share items through a variety of methods, including email, messages, Facebook and X (formerly Twitter). The **Share** button can also be used to share items using the AirDrop function over short distances with other compatible Apple devices (see page 40). To access these options, tap once on this button, where available:

What is an App?

An app is just a more modern name for a computer program. Initially, it was used in relation to mobile devices, such as the iPhone and the iPad, but it is now becoming more widely used with desktop and laptop computers, for both Mac and Windows operating systems.

On the iPad there are two types of apps:

- **Built-in apps**. These are the apps that come pre-installed on the iPad.

- **App Store apps**. These are apps that can be downloaded from the online App Store. There is a huge range of apps available there, covering a variety of different categories. Some are free, while others have to be paid for. The apps in the App Store are updated and added to on a daily basis, so there are always new ones to explore.

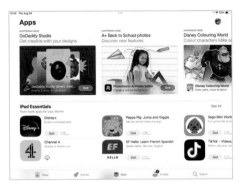

There are also two important points to remember about apps (both built-in and those from the App Store):

- Apart from some of the built-in apps, the majority of apps do not interact with each other. This means that there is less chance of viruses being transmitted from app to app on your iPad, and apps can also operate without a reliance on other apps.

- Content created by apps is saved within the app itself, rather than within a file structure on your iPad – e.g. if you create a note in the Notes app, it is saved there; if you take a photo, it is saved in the Photos app. Content is also usually saved automatically when it is created or edited, so you do not have to worry about saving as you work.

Built-in Apps

The built-in iPad apps are the ones that appear on the Home screen when you turn on the iPad:

Some of the built-in apps appear on the second Home screen of the iPad.

- **App Store**. This can be used to access the App Store, from where additional apps can then be downloaded.

- **Books**. This is an app for downloading electronic books, which can then be read on the iPad. This can be done for both plain text and illustrated items.

You need an Apple ID to obtain content from the **Books** app. Books are downloaded in a matter of seconds. For full details about obtaining an Apple ID, see page 99.

- **Calendar**. An app for storing appointments, important dates and other calendar information. It can be synced with iCloud.

- **Camera**. This gives direct access to the front-facing and rear-facing iPad cameras. You can also access your photo gallery from here.

- **Clock**. This displays the current time and can be used to view the time in different countries, and also as an alarm clock and a stopwatch.

- **Contacts**. An address book app. Once contacts are added here they can then also be accessed from other apps, such as Mail.

- **FaceTime**. This is an app that uses the built-in front-facing camera on the iPad to hold video chats with other people with Apple devices, and also invite people who are using non-Apple devices (Windows or Android).

The iPad **Settings** app is another of the built-in apps, and this is looked at in detail on pages 26-27.

87

...cont'd

- **Files**. This app can be used to display and access files held on your iPad, in iCloud Drive, and in other online file storage services such as Dropbox.

- **Find My**. This is an app that can be used to view the location of anyone who is part of your Family Sharing group in iCloud.

- **Freeform**. This uses a virtual whiteboard, where you can add a range of content, from text to shapes and images.

- **Home**. This can be used to control certain compatible functions within the home, such as heating controls.

- **iTunes Store**. This app can be used to browse the iTunes store, where music, TV shows, movies, and more can be downloaded to your iPad.

- **Mail**. This is the email app for sending and receiving email on your iPad.

- **Maps**. Use this app to view maps from around the world, find specific locations, and get directions to destinations.

- **Measure**. This can be used to measure objects, using the iPad's camera.

- **Messages**. This is the iPad messaging service, which can be used between iPads, iPhones and Mac computers.

- **Music**. An app for playing music on your iPad and also accessing the Apple Music service, which connects to the whole iTunes Library.

- **News**. This is an app that collates news stories and content from numerous sources.

- **Notes**. If you need to jot down your thoughts or ideas, this app is perfect for just that.

- **Photo Booth**. This is an app for creating fun and creative effects with your photos.

- **Photos**. This is an app for viewing and editing photos, creating slideshows, and for viewing videos you have taken with your iPad camera. It can also be used to share photos via iCloud.

- **Podcasts**. This can be used to download and play podcasts from within the App Store.

- **Reminders**. Use this app for organization, when you want to create to-do lists and set reminders for events.

- **Safari**. The Apple web browser that has been developed for viewing the web on your iPad.

- **Stocks**. This can be used to display real-time stock prices and related news from Apple News.

- **Tips**. This can be used to display tips and hints for items on your iPad.

- **Translate**. This can be used to translate a wide range of different languages, including audio conversation options.

- **TV**. This is an app for viewing videos purchased from the Apple TV Store on your iPad, and also streaming them to a larger HDTV monitor.

- **Voice Memos**. This can be used to record and share voice recordings.

- **Weather**. This can be used to display detailed weather information from locations around the world.

It is worth investing in a good pair of headphones for listening to music and podcasts so that you do not disturb other people.

The Health app is also included for the first time on the iPad – this is a new feature in iPadOS 17. See pages 154-155 for details.

About the App Store

While the built-in apps that come with the iPad are flexible and versatile, it really comes into its own when you connect to the App Store. This is an online resource containing thousands of apps that can be downloaded and then used on your iPad, including categories from Lifestyle to Travel.

To use the App Store, you must first have an Apple ID. This can be obtained when you first connect to the App Store. Once you have an Apple ID, you can start exploring the App Store.

For full details about obtaining an Apple ID, see page 99.

Tap once on the **Get** button to download a free app (a paid-for one will display a price).

1 Tap once on the **App Store** app on the Home screen

2 The App Store Homepage (accessed using the **Today** button) displays the latest recommended apps. Swipe up the page to move to other daily recommendations

3 Tap on the buttons on the bottom toolbar to view the options according to **Today**, **Games**, **Apps**, and **Arcade**

The **Arcade** section is a monthly subscription service that contains an extensive range of games.

4 Tap once on an app to view its details

5 Swipe up the page to view more information about the app

Finding Apps

Within the App Store, apps are separated into categories according to type. To find apps in the App Store:

 Tap once on the **Apps** button on the bottom toolbar

 Details of the latest apps are displayed

Some apps will differ depending on the geographical location from where you are accessing the App Store.

 Scroll down the page (by swiping up) to view the different sections. Tap once on the **See All** button to view all items in a section

You can buy bundles of apps from some developers at a reduced price.

Categories

To view the different categories in the App Store:

 Tap once on the **Apps** button on the bottom toolbar

Apps

 Swipe up the page to the **Top Categories** section

Top Categories

Entertainment	Kids
Graphics & Design	Shopping
Safari Extensions	Education

When viewing apps within a specific category, swipe up the page to view **Top Paid** and **Top Free** apps for the category.

 Tap once on the **See All** button to view all available categories. Tap once on a category to view the apps within it

Another way to find apps is with the App Store **Search** button, which is located at the right of the bottom toolbar of the App Store. To use this: tap once on the **Search** button

Q Search

and tap once in the Search box to bring up the iPad virtual keyboard. Enter a search keyword or phrase. Suggestions appear as you are typing. Tap once on a result to view the related app and information about it.

Do not limit yourself to just viewing the top apps. Although these are the most popular, there are also a lot of excellent apps within each category.

...cont'd

Top Charts
To find top-rated apps:

 Tap once on the **Apps** button on the bottom toolbar

 Apps

2 Swipe up the page to view the current **Top Free Apps** and **Top Paid Apps**

3 Tap once on the **See All** button to see the full range of paid-for and free apps

See All

4 Tap once on the **All Apps** button, and tap once on a category to view the **Top Free** and **Top Paid** apps for that category

All Apps

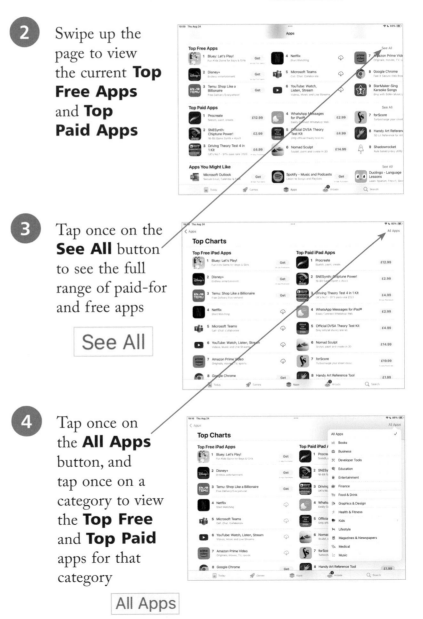

Obtaining Apps

When you identify an app that you would like to use, it can be downloaded to your iPad. To do this:

1 Find the app you want to download, and tap once on the button next to the app (this will say **Get** or will have a price)

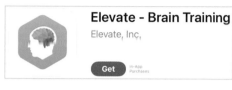

2 Tap once on the **Install** button

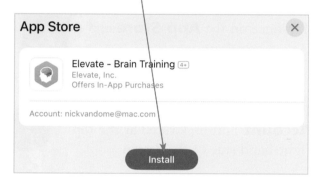

3 The app will begin to download onto your iPad, indicated by this icon next to it in the App Store

4 Once the app is downloaded it will appear in the next available space on one of the Home screens. Tap once on the app to open and use it

Apps usually download in a few minutes or less, depending on the speed of your internet connection.

Some apps have "in-app purchases". This is additional content that has to be paid for when it is downloaded, after the initial download of an app.

To have newly downloaded apps appear only in the App Library and not on the Home screen, go to **Settings** > **Home Screen & App Library** and tap once on the **App Library Only** option in the **Newly Downloaded Apps** section.

You should keep your apps as up-to-date as possible to take advantage of software fixes and updates.

Hot tip

If updates are not set to be downloaded automatically, a notification badge will appear on the App Store icon to indicate that updates are available. These can then be updated in the **Account** section of the App Store, under the **Available Updates** heading.

Hot tip

The notification badge on apps (such as the **App Store** and the **Mail** app) can be turned **On** or **Off** in **Settings > Notifications > [select app]** by dragging the **Badges** button **On** or **Off**.

Updating Apps

The world of apps is a dynamic and fast-moving one, and new apps are being created and added to the App Store on a daily basis. Existing apps are also being updated, to improve their performance, security and functionality. Once you have installed an app from the App Store, it is possible to obtain updates at no extra cost (whether or not the app was paid for). To do this:

1 Set updates to be downloaded automatically: **Settings** > **App Store** > and drag **App Updates** On

2 Tap once on the **App Store** app

3 In the App Store, tap once on the **Account** button, located at the top right-hand side of the screen

4 Tap once on the **Purchased** option

5 Tap once on the **Open** button to open the latest version. (If automatic updates have not been selected, there will be an **Update All** option at the bottom of the window in Step 4 for apps for which there are updates)

Organizing Apps

When you start downloading apps you will probably soon find that you have dozens, if not hundreds, of them. You can move between screens to view all of your apps by swiping left or right with one finger. It is also possible to organize apps into individual folders to make using them more manageable. To do this:

 1 Press on an app until it starts to wobble and a cross appears at the top-left corner

2 Drag the app over another one

3 A folder is created, containing the two apps. The folder is given a default name, usually based on the category of the apps

4 Tap on the folder name, and type a new name if required

5 Tap anywhere on the Home screen, away from the folder, to finish creating it and return to the Home screen. The folder is added to the Home screen. Tap once on this to access items within it

Hot tip

To move an app between screens, press and hold on it until it starts to wobble and a minus sign appears in the corner. Then, drag it to the side of the screen. If there is space on the next screen, the app will be moved to the point at which it is released.

95

Beware

Only top-level folders can be created; i.e. sub-folders cannot be created. Also, one folder cannot be placed within another.

Hot tip

If you want to rename an app folder after it has been created, press and hold on it until it starts to wobble. Then, tap on it once and edit the name, as in Step 4.

Deleting Apps

If you decide that you do not want certain apps anymore, they can be deleted from your iPad. However, they remain in iCloud so that you can reinstall them if you change your mind. This also means that if you delete an app by mistake, you can get it back from the App Store without having to pay for it again. To delete an app:

If you delete an app it will also delete any data that has been compiled with that app, even if you reinstall it from the App Store.

 Press on an app until it starts to wobble and a minus sign appears at the top-left corner

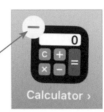

Calculator ›

 Tap once on the minus sign to delete the app. In the Delete dialog box, tap once on the **Delete App** button. The app is then uninstalled from your iPad

Remove "Calculator ›"?
Removing from Home Screen will keep the app in your App Library.

Delete App

Remove from Home Screen

Cancel

To reinstall an app:

In iPadOS 17 some, but not all, of the built-in apps can be deleted. This is done in the same way as deleting an app, shown on this page.

 Tap once on the **App Store** app

App Store

② Tap once on the **Search** button on the bottom toolbar

🔍 Search

③ Enter the name of the app in the Search box, and tap once on the **iCloud** icon to download it again

Calculator & Maths Solver
Scientific and Photo Math Calc
★★★★★ 271K

6 Keeping in Touch

This chapter shows how to use your iPad to keep ahead in the fast-moving world of online communications, using email, a range of texting options, and video chatting with the FaceTime app.

Getting Online

iPads can be used for a variety of different communications, but they all require online access. This is done via Wi-Fi, and you will need to have an Internet Service Provider (ISP) and a Wi-Fi router to connect to the internet. Once this is in place, you will be able to connect to a Wi-Fi network.

Don't forget

If you have the cellular version of the iPad you can obtain internet access this way, but this has to be done through a provider of this service, as with a cell/mobile phone.

1 Tap once on the **Settings** app

2 Tap once on the **Wi-Fi** tab

🛜 Wi-Fi	Off

3 Drag the **Wi-Fi** button to the **On** position

Wi-Fi	⬤

4 Available networks are shown here. Tap once on yours to select it

NETWORKS

PLUSNET-TXJ5	🔒 🛜 ⓘ
PLUSNET-TXJ5-5g	🔒 🛜 ⓘ
Virgin Media	🔒 🛜 ⓘ

Don't forget

If you are connecting to your home Wi-Fi network, the iPad should connect automatically each time, once it has been set up. If you are connecting in a public Wi-Fi area, you will be asked which network you would like to join.

5 Enter the password for your Wi-Fi router

Enter the password for "PLUSNET-TXJ5"

Cancel	**Enter Password**	Join

| Password | •••••••••| |

6 Tap once on the **Join** button   Join

7 Once a network has been joined, a check mark appears next to it. This now provides access to the internet

Wi-Fi	⬤
✓ PLUSNET-TXJ5	🔒 🛜 ⓘ

Obtaining an Apple ID

An Apple ID is an email address and password registered with Apple that enables you to log in and use a variety of online Apple services. These include:

- App Store
- iCloud
- Messages
- FaceTime
- iTunes Store and Apple Music
- Books

It is free to register for an Apple ID, and this can be done when you access one of the apps or services that require it, or you can register on the Apple website at Apple ID (**https://appleid.apple.com**).

Settings > **Apple ID, iCloud, Media & Purchases** is where you can access your Apple ID details.

 Tap once on the **Create Your Apple ID** button at the top of the Apple ID web page

Create Your Apple ID

 Enter details for the **Create Your Apple ID** wizard to set up your Apple ID account. (If you are using an Apple ID to buy items using Apple apps and services, you will need to provide a valid method of payment)

Create Your Apple ID

One Apple ID is all you need to access all Apple services.
Already have an Apple ID? Find it here ›

First name   Last name

COUNTRY / REGION

United States

Birthday

name@example.com

This will be your new Apple ID.

Password

The Apple ID settings (above) also include account recovery options, where you can specify a contact who can be used to recover your Apple ID account details, and also a recovery key that can be used to restore the data on your iPad. Find these at **Settings > Apple ID, iCloud, Media & Purchases > Sign-In & Security > Account Recovery**.

Setting up an Email Account

Email settings can be specified within the Settings app. Different email accounts can also be added. To do this:

Hot tip

If you don't already have an email account set up, you can choose one of the providers from the list and you will be guided through the setup process.

Hot tip

If your email provider is not on the **Add Account** list, tap once on **Other** at the bottom of the list and complete the account details using the information from your email provider.

Don't forget

If you set up more than one email account, messages from all of them can be downloaded and displayed by **Mail**.

1 Tap once on the **Settings** app

Settings

2 Tap once on the **Mail** tab

Mail

3 Tap once on the **Accounts** button

Accounts

4 Tap once on the **Add Account** option to add a new account

< Mail   Accounts

ACCOUNTS
iCloud
iCloud Mail, Contacts, Calendars, Safari, Reminders, Notes, News, Photos and 2 more...

Add Account

5 Tap once on the type of email account you want to add

< Accounts   Add Account

iCloud

Microsoft Exchange

Google

yahoo!

Aol.

Outlook.com

Other

6 Enter your login details for the account. Follow the wizard for the account, and tap on the **Next** button at each stage

Cancel   accounts.google.com   AA

Google
Sign in
Use your Google Account

Let this Mac access your mail and other Google Account data

Email or phone

Forgot email?

Create account   Next

Emailing

Email on the iPad is created, sent and received using the Mail app. To use this:

 1 Tap once on the **Mail** app (the red icon in the corner displays the number of unread emails in your Inbox)

2 Tap once on a message to display it in the main panel. To quickly delete an email from your Inbox, swipe on it from right to left and tap once on the **Trash** (**Delete**) button

3 Use these buttons to, from left to right: reply to the sender; reply to all people in the email (if more than one); forward the email; delete the current message; move the message to another folder; create a new message; and access the Mail app's menu

4 Tap once on this button, at the bottom right of the Mail window, to see options for replying to a message, forwarding it to a new recipient, deleting it, moving it to another folder, or marking it as read or unread

101

Hot tip

Email messages can be unsent for up to 10 seconds after they have been sent. To do this, tap once on the **Undo Send** button at the bottom of the Inbox window.

Undo Send

Hot tip

Use the email settings (**Settings** > **Mail**) to access numerous options for customizing how the Mail app operates.

Don't forget

Once an email has been written, tap once on this button to send it to the recipient:

Don't forget

You need an Apple ID to send iMessages, and have to sign in with it when you start using the Messages app.

Don't forget

iMessages are sent using Wi-Fi. If a Wi-Fi connection is not available, the message cannot be sent, unless the iPad has a cellular network connection.

Don't forget

If an iPad has a cellular network connection, then this can be used to send regular text messages to other compatible devices such as cell/mobile phones. If the recipient is not using iMessages, the message will be sent as a standard SMS (Short Message Service). By default, iMessages appear in blue bubbles and SMS messages in green bubbles.

Text Messaging

Text messaging should not be thought of as the domain of the younger generation. On your iPad you can join the world of text with the Apple iMessage service that is accessed via the Messages app. This enables text, photos, videos, emojis and audio messages to be sent, free of charge, between users of iPadOS on the iPad, iOS on the iPhone, and Mac computers. iMessages can be sent to cell/mobile phone numbers and email addresses.

1 Tap once on the **Messages** app

2 Tap once on this button to create a new message and start a new conversation

3 Tap once on this button to select someone from your contacts

4 Tap once on a contact to select them as the recipient of the new message

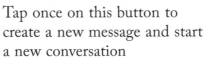

5 Tap once in the text box, and type with the keyboard to create a message. Tap once on this button to send the message

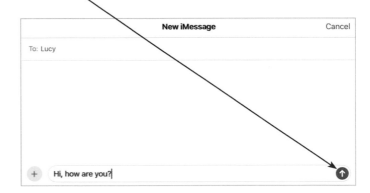

6 As the conversation progresses, each message is displayed in the main window

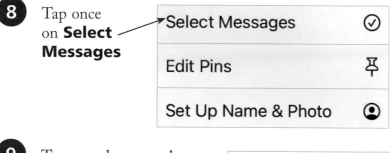

Hot tip

Press and hold on a message, and tap on the **More...** button that appears. Select a message, or messages, and tap on the **Trash** icon to remove it/ them.

7 To edit whole conversations, tap once on the **Edit** button in the Messages panel

Edit

Don't forget

When a message has been sent, you are notified underneath it when it has been delivered.

103

8 Tap once on **Select Messages**

Select Messages ⊘

Edit Pins 📌

Set Up Name & Photo ⓐ

Hot tip

Press and hold on a name in the **Messages** panel and tap once on the **Pin** button to pin this conversation to the top of the panel.

9 Tap once here to select a conversation, and tap once on the **Delete** button at the bottom of the page to delete a conversation

Done

Delete

Pin 📌

Enhancing Text Messages

Adding emojis

Emojis (small graphical symbols) can be used with the Messages app.

Tap once on this button on the keyboard to view the emoji keyboard

Swipe left and right to view the emoji options. Tap once on an emoji to add it to a message

iMessages can also be sent with certain animated effects.

Write a message and press and hold on this button

Tap once on the **Bubble** button at the top of the window, and tap once on one of the options. These are **Slam**, which creates a message that moves in at speed from the side of the screen; **Loud**, which creates a message in large text; **Gentle**, which creates a message in small text; and **Invisible Ink**, which creates a message that is concealed and then reveals the text

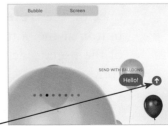

Repeat Step 1 for bubble effects and tap once on the **Screen** button at the top of the window. Swipe left and right to view the full-screen effects. Tap once on this button to send the message

---

Don't forget

Emojis can be added automatically to replace certain words. Add text, and tap once on the **Emoji** button in the first Step 1. Any items that can be replaced by an emoji are highlighted. Tap once on a highlighted word to add an emoji.

Editing and Unsending

When sending text iMessages from an iPad using iPadOS 17 it is possible to edit messages with any mistakes in them, and also unsend a message if it has been sent in error or contains something that you didn't mean to include, although there is a time limit for these operations.

Editing an iMessage

1. Press and hold on a message once it has been sent and tap once on the **Edit** button

Just testing something - ignore this!

Delivered

Edit

2. Edit the message as required and tap once on this icon (the check mark symbol)

Just testing something!

Delivered

3. The edited text is displayed in the conversation window

Just testing something!

Delivered · Edited

Unsending an iMessage

1. Press and hold on a message once it has been sent and tap once on the **Undo Send** button

Undo Send

2. A message is displayed to indicate that the message has been unsent

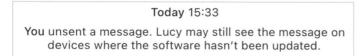

Today 15:33

You unsent a message. Lucy may still see the message on devices where the software hasn't been updated.

Don't forget

iMessages can be edited up to five times within 15 minutes of them being sent. They can be unsent within two minutes of being sent.

Beware

Editing and unsending iMessages is only effective if they are sent to other people using iPadOS 16 or later (or iOS 16 or later for an iPhone and macOS Ventura or later for a Mac computer). If not, the editing and unsending operations may not work and the recipient will just see the original message.

The Plus button, and its features, is a new feature in iPadOS 17.

The features related to the Plus button work best when messages are being sent to other Apple users, using an iPad, iPhone or a Mac computer. Some of the features will not work if you are sending messages to non-Apple users – i.e. those using Android devices – or if the devices have earlier versions of the relevant Apple operating systems.

Messages Plus Button

In iPadOS 17, the new Plus button, next to the Messages text box, can be used to add a variety of useful and fun content to text messages sent from this app. To do this:

1 Tap once on this button (**Plus** button) at the left-hand side of the Messages app text box

2 The main options are displayed. These are: **Camera**, for taking a photo to add it to a message; **Photos**, for adding photos from your Photos app library; **Stickers** (see next page); **Audio**, for sending a voice note (see page 108); and **Location**, for sending someone your current location (see page 109). Tap once on the **More** button for additional options

📷	Camera
✿	Photos
🌙	Stickers
ᇞ	Audio
◉	Location
⌄	More

3 The additional options include: downloading compatible apps and their content, from the **Store** button; **#images**, which are animated GIF images; creating graphical images with **Digital Touch**; and **Music** for adding music from your Music app

🅐	Store
🔍	#images
◉	Digital Touch
🎵	Music

Creating stickers

Graphical stickers are increasingly used in text messages, and with iPadOS 17 you can create customized stickers, based on your own photos. To do this:

1 Tap once on the **Stickers** button in Step 2 on the previous page

2 Tap once on this button and tap once on the **New Sticker** option in the Stickers drawer

No Stickers
Stickers you create from photos will appear here.
New Sticker

3 Navigate to a photo to use for the sticker, using the top toolbar, and tap on it once

Photos
Q Photos, People, Places...
All Types · Live · People · Animals · Food

4 The background is removed, leaving the main image as the sticker. Tap once on the **Add Sticker** button to add the sticker to the drawer in Step 2. These types of stickers are known as Live Stickers

New Sticker
Cancel   Add Sticker

Being able to create your own customized stickers is a new feature in iPadOS 17.

Don't forget

Once stickers have been added they are available in the drawer in Step 2. Tap once on a sticker to add it to a message. This drawer can also be accessed when adding emojis.

Once a sticker has been added initially, tap once on the **+** button to create more stickers. The Stickers drawer is available in different apps, whenever this icon is available.

Transcribed voice notes is a new feature in iPadOS 17.

Don't forget

Tap once on the **x** button in Step 3 to delete the current voice note before it is sent.

Don't forget

Voice notes can also be created by pressing and holding on this button at the right-hand side of the Messages text box, before a message has been started, and recording a message:

...cont'd

Adding voice notes

Voice notes are becoming a popular addition to text messages, whereby an audio message is created for the recipient to listen to. In iPadOS 17 this is taken one step further: voice notes are also transcribed when they are delivered so that the recipient can read the message first and then listen to the voice note at a later time, if required. To create a voice note and its transcription:

1 Tap once on the **Audio** button in Step 2 on page 106

2 The recording option starts automatically. Speak your voice note and tap once here to complete it

3 Tap once here to send the voice note

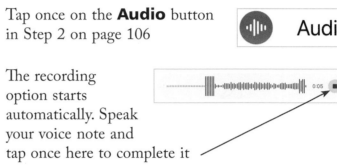

4 The recipient receives the audio file containing the voice note. They can access the voice note by

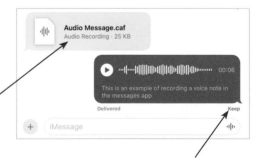

tapping on the audio file. The transcribed version of the voice note is displayed on your own side of the conversation. Tap once on the **Keep** button to retain the message so that the recipient can still see the transcription of the voice note

Sharing your location

With iPadOS 17 you can send people details of your current location, and even send them directions. To do this:

 1 Tap once on the **Location** button in Step 2 on page 106

Sending your location through the Messages app is a new feature in iPadOS 17.

2 Your current location is displayed on a map. Tap once on the **Share** button and select an option for how long you want to share your location

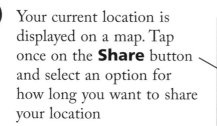

SHARE MY LOCATION	
Indefinitely	∞
Until End of Day	📅
For One Hour	⏲

Hot tip

It is also possible to request someone else's location, if they want to give it to you. To do this, tap once on the **Request** button in Step 2 and the recipient will then be able to send their location via the message they receive.

3 The duration of sharing selected in Step 2 is shown in the top left-hand corner. Tap once on this button to send the message and share your location

Request

4 The recipient receives a copy of the map with your Apple ID image and your location. There is also a **Directions** button, which they can use to get directions to your location

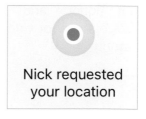

Nick requested your location

Video Chatting with FaceTime

Video chatting is a very personal and interactive way to keep in touch with family and friends around the world. To use FaceTime for video chatting:

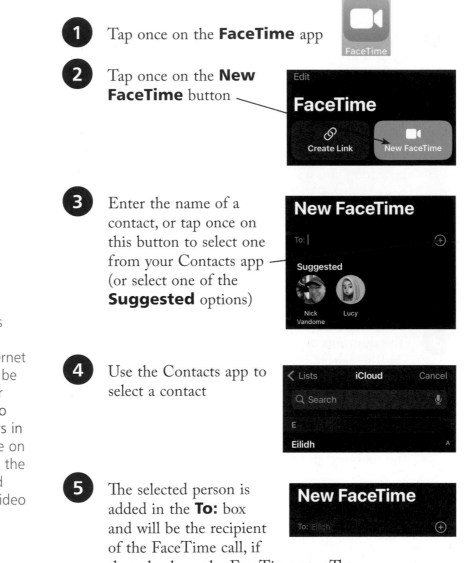

1 Tap once on the **FaceTime** app

2 Tap once on the **New FaceTime** button

3 Enter the name of a contact, or tap once on this button to select one from your Contacts app (or select one of the **Suggested** options)

4 Use the Contacts app to select a contact

5 The selected person is added in the **To:** box and will be the recipient of the FaceTime call, if they also have the FaceTime app. The **Create Link** button in Step 2 can be used to make FaceTime calls to anyone who does not have the FaceTime app – see page 113

110

Don't forget

To make video calls with FaceTime you need an active internet connection and to be signed in with your Apple ID. See Video Chatting for Seniors in easy steps for more on getting connected, the right etiquette, and other options for video chatting.

6 If a contact has the FaceTime app, tap once on the **FaceTime** button to start a video call with them

7 When you have connected, your contact appears in the main window and you appear in a **Picture in Picture** thumbnail in the corner

8 Use these buttons during a call to, from left to right: turn the speakers on or off; turn the camera on or off for the call (audio will still be available if the camera is off); mute or unmute the microphone; share your screen; and end the call

9 Tap once on the **FaceTime** option in Step 8 to access more options for the call, including, from top to bottom: ending the call; adding more people to the call; sharing links to the call for non-FaceTime users; and silencing requests from other people to join a FaceTime call

Hot tip

The **Share Link** option in Step 9 can be used to create FaceTime calls with non-FaceTime users, including those using the Windows and Android operating systems. See page 113 for details.

111

...cont'd

Receiving a FaceTime call

To answer a FaceTime call made to you by someone else:

By default, when you receive a FaceTime call it appears as a small banner at the top of the screen, if the iPad is unlocked. This can be changed to a full-screen image of the caller, in Settings > FaceTime > Incoming Calls > Full Screen.

1 If the iPad is unlocked, tap once the green video button to accept the call, or tap once on the red button to decline the call. If the **Accept** button is selected, tap once on the **Join** button

2 If the iPad is locked, swipe the **slide to answer** button to the right to connect the call

3 Tap once on the **Message** button above to send a text message instead of answering a call, or the **Remind Me** button to set a reminder

Microphone modes

FaceTime also has options for how the microphone operates.

Spatial sound is used in group calls to present the sound as coming from the direction of the screen in which someone's FaceTime window is positioned, to create a more natural effect. This is available on iPads with the A12 Bionic chip, and later.

1 Start a FaceTime call, access the Control Center (see page 38) and tap once on the **Mic Mode** button

Mic Mode
Standard

2 Tap once on the **Voice Isolation** button to block out background noise and give clearer prominence to the current speaker in a call

FaceTime

Standard

Voice Isolation ✓

Wide Spectrum

Creating a FaceTime link

FaceTime can also be used to send a link to anyone, who can then join the FaceTime call via the web, even if they do not have their own FaceTime app. This can include users who do not have an Apple device, and so it is an excellent option for including Android users. To do this:

1 Open the FaceTime app and tap once on the **Create Link** button

It is also possible to invite someone to an existing FaceTime call, via a link, using the **Share Link** button in Step 9 on page 111.

2 Select an option for how you want to send a link to join the FaceTime call – e.g. by email

When someone receives an invitation to a FaceTime call, the recipient can tap once on the **FaceTime Link** button in the invitation, enter their name and tap once on the **Continue** button.

3 Compose an invitation in the app selected in Step 2 and send it to the recipient

113

...cont'd

Using SharePlay in FaceTime

SharePlay is a function within FaceTime that enables you to share your screen and play movies, TV shows and music, and share this content with other people on a FaceTime call. To do this:

1 Access **Settings** > **FaceTime** > **SharePlay** and drag the **SharePlay** button **On**

2 To share your screen, start a FaceTime call and tap once on this button on the FaceTime control panel to share your iPad screen with everyone else on an existing call

3 Tap once on the **Share My Screen** button

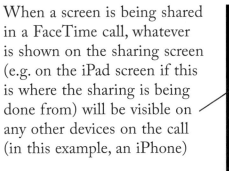

4 When a screen is being shared in a FaceTime call, whatever is shown on the sharing screen (e.g. on the iPad screen if this is where the sharing is being done from) will be visible on any other devices on the call (in this example, an iPhone)

Sharing music, movies or TV shows

SharePlay can also be used to share content with other people on a FaceTime call from the Music app and the TV app. To do this:

 Start a FaceTime call and access the sharing options as shown on the previous page. Tap once on the **TV** icon or the **Music** icon

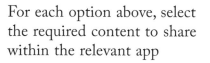 For each option above, select the required content to share within the relevant app

 Don't forget

Content for SharePlay is synchronized for everyone in a FaceTime call, so everyone sees and hears the same content at the same time.

For the **TV** app, select how you want to use an item you are opening – e.g. use it with SharePlay so that people on the FaceTime call can see it, or just open it for yourself on your iPad

Content from the **TV** app that is used with SharePlay plays within the FaceTime interface, and everyone on the call will be able to view it at the same time. Before joining the shared content, the recipient has to accept the SharePlay invitation, by tapping once on the **Open** button

Don't forget

If you have instigated a sharing session, when you want to end it you can specify this for only yourself, or everyone on the sharing session.

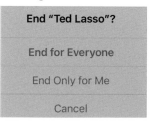

Adding Social Media

Using social media sites such as Facebook, Instagram and X (formerly known as Twitter) to keep in touch with family and friends has now become common across all generations. On the iPad it is possible to download a range of social media apps and also view updates through the Notification Center. To add social media apps:

Don't forget

Within the App Store there is a range of social media and communication apps that can be used to contact friends and family via text, phone and video. There are also several apps for sharing information, updates and photos. Some of these are: **Facebook**; **X** (formerly known as Twitter); **Snapchat**; **Instagram**; **Flickr**; **Skype**; **Zoom**; **WordPress**, for web publishing; and **Gmail** for online webmail that can be linked to your iPad with the Mail app.

1 Open the App Store and navigate to the **Apps** > **Categories** > **Social Networking** section

2 Tap once on the required apps to download them to your iPad

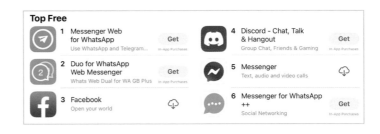

3 Tap once on an app to open it

4 If you already have an account with the social media service, enter your login details, or tap once on the **Sign up for Facebook** button to create a new account

7 On a Web Safari

This chapter shows how to use the functionality of the built-in iPad web browser, Safari, to access the web and start enjoying the benefits of the online world.

Around Safari

The Safari app is the default web browser on the iPad. This can be used to view web pages, bookmark pages, and read pages with the **Reader** function. To start using Safari:

1 Tap once on the **Safari** app

2 Tap once on the Address Bar at the top of the Safari window. Type a name or a web page address

3 Tap once on the **Go** button on the keyboard to open the web page that was entered, or select one of the options below the Address Bar

go

Don't forget

The Safari Address Bar, and top toolbars, take on the color of the web page being viewed, extending the web page to the edge of the window.

4 The selected page opens with the top toolbar visible. As you swipe up the page, this disappears to give you a greater viewing area. Tap on the top of the screen, or swipe back down, to display the toolbar again

5 Swipe up and down and left and right to navigate around the page

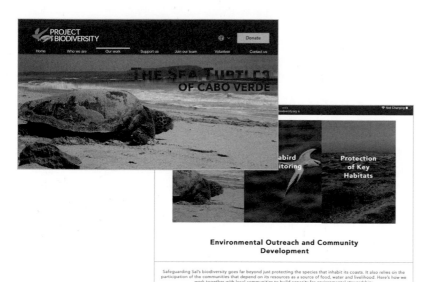

6 Swipe outward with thumb and forefinger to zoom in on a web page (pinch inward to zoom back out)

Don't forget

When a page opens in Safari, a blue status bar underneath the Address Bar indicates the progress of the loading page.

Don't forget

Double-tap with one finger to zoom in on a page by a set amount. Double-tap again with one finger to return to normal view. If the page has been zoomed by a greater amount by pinching, double-tap with two fingers to return to normal view.

Hot tip

Other browsers can be downloaded from the App Store. Some to try are: Google Chrome, Firefox, and Opera Browser.

Beware

If other people have access to your iPad, don't use **AutoFill** for names and passwords for any sites with sensitive information, such as banking sites.

Hot tip

If the **Open New Tabs in Background** option in Step 4 is set to **On**, you can press and hold a link on a web page and select **Open in New Tab**. The link then opens in a new tab behind the one you are viewing.

Don't forget

Cookies are small items from websites that obtain details from your browser when you visit a site. The cookie remembers the details for the next time you visit the site.

Safari Settings

Settings for Safari can be specified in the Settings app.

1 Open the Settings app and tap once on the **Safari** tab

Safari

2 Tap once on the **Search Engine** link to select a default search engine to use

Search Engine

3 Tap once here for options for filling in online forms

GENERAL

AutoFill

4 Drag this button **On** to open new pages in the background of your current page

Open New Tabs in Background

5 Drag this button **On** to keep the Favorites Bar in view under the Address Bar in Safari

Show Favorites Bar

6 Drag the **Advanced** > **Block All Cookies** button **On** or **Off** as required

Block All Cookies

7 Tap once on **Clear History and Website Data** to remove these

Clear History and Website Data

8 Drag this button **On** to enable alerts for when you visit a fraudulent website

Fraudulent Website Warning

9 Drag this button **On** to block pop-up messages

Block Pop-ups

Navigating Pages

When you are viewing pages within Safari there are a number of functions that can be used.

 1 Tap once on these arrows to move forward and back between web pages that have been visited

2 Tap once on this button to view or hide the contents of the left-hand sidebar (see page 122)

3 Tap once here to add a bookmark (see page 123); add to a Reading List; add an icon to your iPad Home screen; email a link to a page; share using social media, messaging and other apps; or print a page

4 Tap once here to open a new tab (see page 125)

5 Tap and hold a link to access additional options, including: **Open**; **Open in Background**; **Open in Tab Group**; **Open in New Window**; **Download Linked File**; **Add to Reading List**; **Copy Link**; and **Share...** using a selection of options

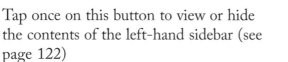

Open	⊘
Open in Background	⊞
Open in Tab Group	↗
Open in New Window	⊞
Download Linked File	⊙
Add to Reading List	∞
Copy Link	⧉
Share...	⬆

 6 Tap and hold on an image, and tap once on **Share...**, **Save to Photos** or **Copy**

Share...	⬆
Save to Photos	⬇
Copy	⧉

Hot tip

Tap and hold on the **Forward** and **Back** arrows in Step 1 to view lists of previously-visited pages in these directions. See page 123 for more on bookmarking.

Hot tip

Files can be downloaded from Safari and then viewed in the Files app, from the **Downloads** button in the sidebar. To do this, press and hold on a link on a web page to the file you want to download, and tap once on the **Download Linked File** button.

Download Linked File	⊙

Sidebar

The Safari sidebar can be used to manage tabs within Safari, use private browsing, and also view items that have been saved within Safari. To use the sidebar:

Hot tip

Tap once on this button in the top right-hand corner of the sidebar to access options for creating a new, empty tab group or one from existing tabs.

| New Empty Tab Group | |
| New Tab Group from 5 Tabs | |

1 Tap once here to view or hide the sidebar

2 Tap once on the **Tabs** button to view all currently-open tabs in Safari

3 Tap once on the **Private** button to access web pages without any browsing data being recorded or stored

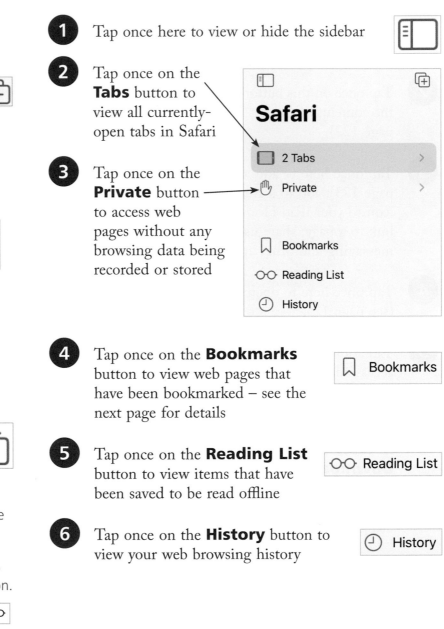

Hot tip

To add an item to the Reading List, access the required web pages and tap once on this button on the top toolbar to access sharing options. Tap once on the **Add to Reading List** button.

| Add to Reading List | ∞ |

4 Tap once on the **Bookmarks** button to view web pages that have been bookmarked – see the next page for details

5 Tap once on the **Reading List** button to view items that have been saved to be read offline

6 Tap once on the **History** button to view your web browsing history

Bookmarking Pages

Once you start using Safari, you will soon build up a collection of favorite pages that you visit regularly. To access these quickly, they can be bookmarked so that you can go to them in one tap. To set up and use bookmarks:

 Open a web page that you want to bookmark. Tap once on this button on the top toolbar to access sharing options

123

2 Tap once on the **Add Bookmark** button

Hot tip

For pages that you access frequently, you can also choose **Add to Home Screen** from the sharing options in Step 2 (swipe up the panel to access this option).

3 Tap once in this box to select whether to include the bookmark on the Favorites bar or in a Bookmarks folder

4 Tap once on the **Save** button

5 On the web page, tap once on this button to access the sidebar. Tap once on the **Bookmarks** button to view all bookmarks that have been added

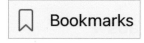

Tab View

Tabs can be managed using iPadOS 17 on the iPad so that you can view all of your open Safari tabs on one screen, including those on other compatible Apple devices. To do this:

Hot tip

Tab View can also be activated by pinching inward with thumb and forefinger on a web page that is at normal magnification; i.e. 1 to 1.

Don't forget

Tap once on the **Done** button at the top of the Tab View window to exit this and return to the web page that was being viewed when Tab View was activated.

Done

1 Tap once here to activate **Tab View**

2 All currently-open tabs are displayed. Tap on one to open it

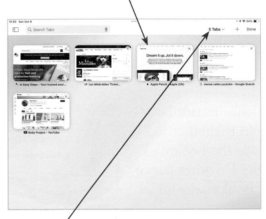

3 Tap once on the **Tab Groups** button on the top toolbar to access options for viewing **Private** tabs and also for creating new tab groups

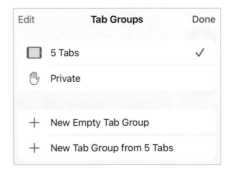

Opening New Tabs

Safari supports tabbed browsing, which means that you can open separate pages within the same window and access them by tapping on each tab at the top of the page.

Hot tip

Items that appear in the Start Page window can be determined by tapping once on the **Edit** button toward the bottom of the window and making selections as required.

 1 Tap once here to open a new tab for another page

 2 Open a new page by entering a web address into the Address Bar, or tap on one of the thumbnails in the **Start Page** window

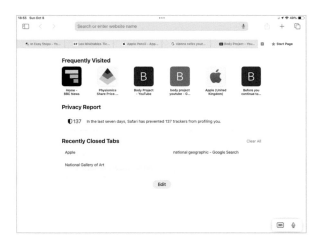

Don't forget

Press and hold on this button to access options for opening a new tab, opening a new private tab, or closing all currently-open tabs:

Halifax ...

3 Tap once on the tab headings to move between tabbed pages

Hot tip

If there are too many items to be displayed on the Favorites Bar, tap once on this button to view the other items.

4 Tap once on the cross to the top left of a tab to close the active tab

Web Page Options

Being able to view web pages in the way that you want is an important part of any browsing experience, and Safari offers various options for displaying web pages. These can be accessed from the left-hand side of the Address Bar.

Don't forget

In Reader View, the button in the Address Bar turns black. Tap once on it to access options for how Reader View is displayed, including text size, background color and font. It can also be used to hide Reader View and return to the full web page.

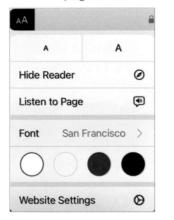

1 Tap once on this button in the Address Bar

2 The web page options are displayed

3 Tap once on these buttons to change the text size of a web page

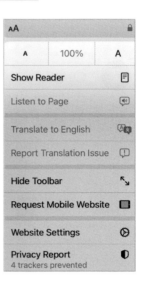

4 Tap once on the **Show Reader** button, if available, to view the current web page with just text and no extra content, such as adverts

5 Tap once on the **Hide Toolbar** button to hide the toolbar and create a larger viewing area for the current web page

6 Tap once on the **Request Mobile Website** button to view a mobile version of the website, if there is one

7 Tap once on the **Website Settings** button to access settings for the website being viewed

8 Tap once on the **Privacy Report** button to view details of items that have been blocked

8 Staying Organized

An iPad is ideal for organizational tasks. This chapter shows how to use it to keep fully up-to-date.

Taking Notes

It is always useful to have a quick way of making notes of everyday things, such as shopping lists, recipes or packing lists. On your iPad, the Notes app is perfect for this.

1 Tap once on the **Notes** app

2 Tap once on this button to create a new note

3 Tap once in the text area of a new note to access the keyboard. Start writing the note

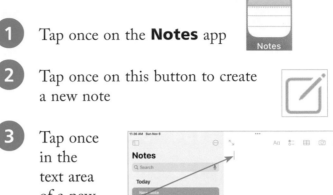

Formatting notes

To apply a range of formatting to a note:

If iCloud is set up for Notes (check **Notes** is **On** in **Settings** > **Apple ID iCloud, Media & Purchases** > **iCloud**) then all of your notes will be stored here and will be available on any other iCloud-enabled devices that you have.

1 Tap once on the yellow cursor to activate the selection handles

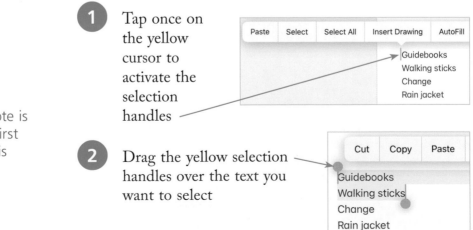

The title for a note is taken from the first line of text that is entered.

2 Drag the yellow selection handles over the text you want to select

3 Tap once on the **Formatting** button on the top toolbar to access formatting options, including text styles such as **Title**, **Heading** or **Body** options, or list options for creating a list from the selection

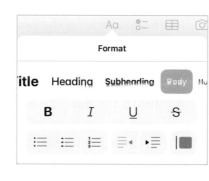

Options for formatting text in a note are located on the Shortcuts bar, below the main text window, and on the top toolbar.

4 Tap once on the **List** button on the top toolbar to create a checklist from the selected text. Radio buttons are added to the list (these are the round buttons to the left-hand side of the text). Tap once on the radio buttons to show that an item or a task has been completed

Items in a list can be set to automatically move to the bottom of the list once they have been completed. To do this, go to **Settings > Notes > Sort Checked Items** and tap once on the **Automatically** option.

5 Tap once on the **Camera** button on the top toolbar and tap once on the **Take Photo or Video** button to add a photo or a video to the note, or tap once on the **Choose Photo or Video** button to add a photo from the iPad's photo library

Take Photo or Video	📷
Scan Documents	📄
Choose Photo or Video	🖼

Tap once on this button on the Shortcuts bar to insert a table into a note:

129

...cont'd

Tap once on the menu button in the top right-hand corner of the Notes panel to access a menu for managing your notes, including: changing the Notes window view; selecting notes; sorting and grouping notes; and viewing any attachments that have been added to notes.

View as Gallery	🔲
Select Notes	⊘
Sort By Default (Date Edited)	↕ >
Group By Date Default (On)	🗔 >
View Attachments	📎

Notes can also be deleted by swiping from right to left on them in the Notes panel and tapping once on the Trash icon.

🗑

6 Tap once on the **Add Sketch** button on the top toolbar to add a freehand sketch to a note. Click on the pen and color options as required

7 Tap once on this button on the keyboard to hide the keyboard and finish the note. To edit an existing note, tap once on the text and the keyboard will reappear

Managing notes

Once notes have been created they can be managed from within their own window. To do this:

1 In the main **Notes** window, tap once on the menu button, at the right-hand side of the top toolbar

2 Tap once on the menu options to apply them. These include options for: scanning items into a note; pinning a note; locking a note; or deleting it. There are also options for: searching for items; moving a note to a folder within the Notes app; applying lines and grids over a note; debugging a note (finding any computer coding errors in a note); and customizing the Notes toolbar

🔲 Scan	📌 Pin	🔒 Lock
Find in Note		🔍
Move Note		🗁
Lines & Grids		⊞
Attachment View		🔲 >
Delete		🗑
Debug		🐞 >
Customize Toolbar		🔧

Pinning notes

By default, the most recently-created or -edited note appears at the top of the **Notes** panel. However, it is possible to pin your most frequently-used notes to the top of this panel. To do this:

1 Press and hold on the note to be pinned

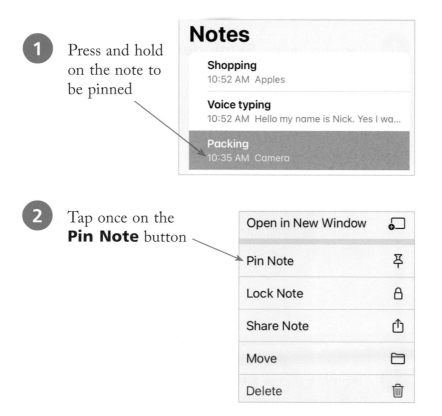

Notes can also be created from within any other app without having to open the Notes app separately. This is known as Quick Notes. Once these have been created, they are all stored in the Notes app. To create and manage Quick Notes: from within any compatible app, swipe inward from the bottom right-hand corner of the iPad. The Quick Note panel appears. Enter text for the Quick Note and tap once on the **Done** button. Tap once on the Notes app to view the Quick Note.

2 Tap once on the **Pin Note** button

3 The note is pinned at the top of the Notes panel. Tap once here to show or hide pinned notes

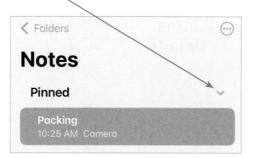

To unpin a note, press and hold on it and tap once on the **Unpin Note** button.

Setting Reminders

Another useful organization app is Reminders. This enables you to create lists for different topics and then set reminders for specific items. A date and time can be set for each reminder, and when this is reached, the reminder appears on your iPad screen. To use Reminders:

Hot tip

Reminders is one of the apps that can also be used with the online iCloud service, which is provided once you have an Apple ID. This is accessed at **www.icloud.com** Other apps that can be accessed here include Contacts, Calendar and Notes.

Hot tip

If Family Sharing has been set up (see page 67 for details), you can create a family reminder that will appear for all members of your Family Sharing group. To do this, tap once on the **Family** button in Step 2 and add a reminder in the usual way.

1 Tap once on the **Reminders** app

2 Items that have been created are listed under specific categories and beneath the **My Lists** heading. This includes reminders and lists. Tap once on this button to reorder or delete any of the lists

3 Tap once on the **Reminders** option and tap once on the **New Reminder** button

4 Enter text for the reminder and tap once on the **i** button to access the **Details** window

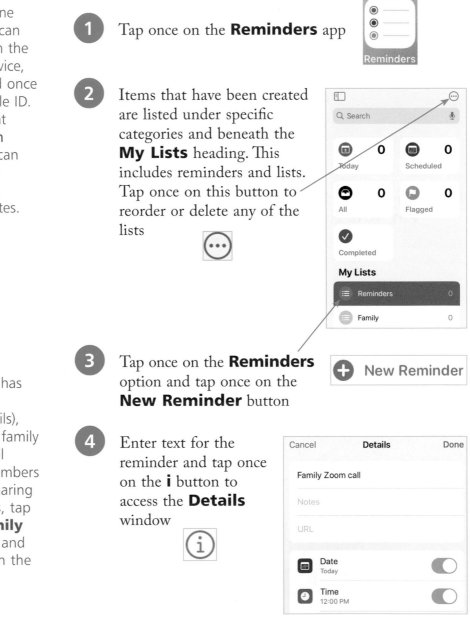

5 Drag the **Date** or **Time** buttons **On** and select options for relevant items for the reminder

6 Tap once on the **Done** button in Step 4 on the previous page to create the reminder

7 On the date and time of the reminder, a pop-up box appears

8 Press and hold on the reminder to access its menu options. Tap once on **Mark as Completed** to close the reminder, or select an option for being reminded about it

Mark as Completed	◉
Remind Me in an Hour	🕐
Remind Me This Afternoon	🕐
Remind Me Tomorrow	🗓

9 Tap once on the **Today** and **Scheduled** buttons at the top left-hand side of the main app window (shown in Step 2 on the previous page) to see reminders and lists for these categories. Appropriate items will be added automatically to these categories

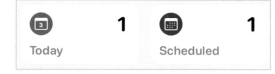

 Hot tip

For a recurring reminder, tap once on the **Repeat** link, further down the window in Step 5, and select a repeat option from: **Never**, **Hourly**, **Daily**, **Weekly**, **Biweekly**, **Monthly**, **Every 3 Months**, **Every 6 Months**, or **Yearly**. The reminder will then appear at the specified time and date set in Step 5.

133

Using the Calendar

The built-in iPad calendar can be used to create and view appointments and events. To do this:

The iPad calendar uses continuous scrolling to move through **Month** view. This means you can view weeks across different months, rather than just viewing each month in its entirety.

1 Tap once on the **Calendar** app

2 By default, the calendar is displayed in **Month** view. Swipe up and down to move between weeks and months

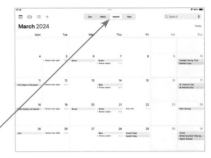

Tap once on these buttons in the top left-hand corner of the calendar window to, from left to right: view available calendars; view invitations; and view the calendar sidebar:

3 Tap once here to view the calendar by **Day**, **Week**, **Month** or **Year** view

Day	Week	Month	Year

4 Tap once on the **Today** button to view the current date

Today

5 Tap once on this button to create a new event, or press and hold on a different date to add an event here

$+$

6 Enter a title and a location for the event

Drag the **All-day** button **On** to set an event for the whole day.

7 Drag the **All-day** button **Off** to set a timescale for the event

Cancel	New Event	Add

Zoo visit

Location or Video Call

All-day

Starts	Mar 22, 2024	11:00
Ends	Mar 22, 2024	12:00

All-day

8 Tap on the **Starts** and **Ends** dates to set these by dragging on the time barrels

Cancel	New Event	Add
Zoo visit		
Location or Video Call		
All-day		◯
Starts	Mar 22, 2024	11:00
Ends	Mar 22, 2024	16:00

```
        13      45
        14      50
        15      55
        16      00
        17      05
        18      10
```

A new event can also be created in **Day** view. Press and hold on a time slot to access the **New Event** window.

Hot tip

9 To invite other people to the event, tap once on the **Invitees** link (**Calendars** needs to be **On** in iCloud for this function)

Invitees	None ›

10 Tap once on this button to select a contact from your address book

Cancel	Add Invitees	Done
To:		⊕

Tap once on the **Repeat** link in the **New Event** window to set a recurring event, such as a birthday. The repeat options are **Every Day**, **Every Week**, **Every 2 Weeks**, **Every Month**, or **Every Year**.

Hot tip

11 The contact is added as an invitee for the event

Cancel	Add Invitees	Done
To: Eilidh		⊕

12 Tap once on the **Done** button. An email invitation will then be sent to the invitee's email address

13 Tap once on the **Add** button shown in the image for Step 6 on the previous page when you have finished entering details of the event

14 Press and hold on an event, and tap on the **Edit** button to alter details of the event

Zoo visit	Edit
Friday, Mar 22, 2024	11:00 to 16:00

Select an event to edit as in Step 14, and tap once on the **Delete Event** button at the bottom of the window to remove it.

Don't forget

Delete Event

135

Your iPad Address Book

There is a built-in address book on your iPad: the Contacts app. This enables you to store contact details, which can then be used to contact people via email, iMessage or FaceTime. To add contacts:

1 Tap once on the **Contacts** app

2 Tap once on this button to add a new contact

3 Enter the required details for a contact

Don't forget

The details of an individual contact can be shared via email or as an iMessage, using the **Share Contact** button at the bottom of their entry.

4 Tap once on the **Done** button

Done

5 Use these buttons to send a text message, make a call, start a FaceTime video call or send an email to a contact

6 Tap once on the **Edit** button to edit details in an individual entry

Edit

7 To delete a contact, swipe to the bottom of the window in **Edit** mode and tap once on the **Delete Contact** button

Delete Contact

Printing Items

Printing from an iPad has its advantages and disadvantages. One advantage is that it is done wirelessly, so you do not have to worry about connecting wires and cables to a printer. The main disadvantage is that not all printers work with the iPad printing system.

AirPrint

Content from an iPad is printed using the AirPrint system that is part of the iPadOS 17 operating system. This is a wireless printing system that connects to your printer through your Wi-Fi network. However, not all printers are AirPrint- or Wi-Fi-enabled, so it may not work with your current printer.

AirPrint can print content from apps with the **Share** button, including built-in apps like Safari, Notes, Mail, and Photos.

Check on the Apple website for a list of AirPrint-enabled printers: https://support.apple.com/en-us/HT201311

1. Tap once on the **Share** button and tap once on the **Print** button

2. Tap once here to select your AirPrint printer

3. Select options for the number of copies, double- or single-sided, and color, then tap once on the **Print** button

Organization Apps

In the App Store there is a wide range of productivity and organization apps. Some of these are:

Most organization apps are found in the **Productivity** category of the App Store.

Other productivity and organization apps to look at include: Notability; Alarmed; AnyList: Grocery Shopping List; OfficeSuite; iA Writer; Smartsheet; and GoodReader PDF Editor & Viewer.

- **Evernote**. One of the most popular note-taking apps. You can create individual notes and also save them into notebook folders. Evernote works across multiple devices, so if it is installed on other computers or mobile devices, you can access your notes wherever you are.

- **Popplet**. This is a note-taking app that enables you to link notes together so that you can form a mindmap-type creation. You can also include photos and draw pictures.

- **Dropbox**. This is an online service for storing and accessing files. You can upload files from your iPad and then access them from other devices with an internet connection.

- **Bamboo Paper**. This is another note-taking app, but it allows you to do this by handwriting rather than typing. The free version comes with one notebook into which you can put your notes, and the paid-for version provides another 20.

- **Pages**. This is a powerful word processing app that has been developed by Apple. It can be used to create and save documents, which can then be printed or shared via email. There are a number of templates on which documents can be based. There is also a range of formatting and content options.

- **Keynote**. Another Apple productivity app, this is a presentation app that can be used to create slides, which can then be run as a presentation.

- **Numbers**. This is the spreadsheet app that is part of the same suite as Pages and Keynote. Again, templates are provided, or you can create your spreadsheets from scratch to keep track of expenditure or household bills, for instance. You can enter formulas into cells to perform simple or complicated calculations.

(9) Leisure Time

The possibilities for enjoyment from your iPad are huge. This chapter looks at listening to music, capturing and editing photos, reading books, and keeping up with the news. It also covers some lifestyle apps including art, health, cookery, and games.

Buying Music and More

As well as using the Music app (see pages 142-143), music on the iPad can also be accessed using the iTunes Store, using your Apple ID with credit or debit card details added. Music can then be played via the Music app.

1   Tap once on the **iTunes Store** app

2   Tap once on the **Music** button on the iTunes toolbar at the bottom of the window

3   Swipe up and down to view the featured items, or tap once on the **Genres** button to find items this way

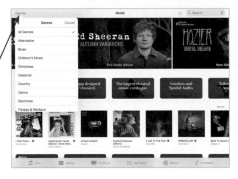

4   Tap once on an item to view it. Tap once here to buy an album, or tap on the price button next to a song to buy that individual item

5   Purchased items are included in the Music app's Library (see pages 142-143) as well as the iTunes Library, from where they can be downloaded again at any time to your iPad or any other Apple device

Around the iTunes Store

In addition to music, there is a wide range of other content that can be downloaded from the iTunes Store.

 Tap once on the **Movies/Films** button to view the latest movie releases

 Tap once on the **TV Shows/TV Programmes** button to view the latest TV releases

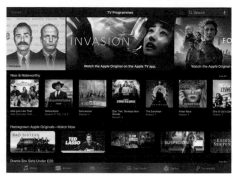

Tap once on the **Top Charts** button on the bottom toolbar to view top-selling items for music, movies and TV

Tap once on the **Genius** button on the bottom toolbar to view suggestions made by iTunes based on your previous purchases

Tap once on the **Purchased** button on the bottom toolbar to view all of your previous purchases from the iTunes Store

Don't forget

Swipe up and down to view the content on the Homepage for Movies and TV. Swipe left and right on individual panels to view the items in each section. Tap once on the **See All** button at the top of a panel – e.g. **Recent Releases** – to view all items within it.

141

Hot tip

Since all items that you buy and download from the iTunes Store are kept within the **Purchased** section, if you ever delete or lose an item you can download it again, for free, from this section. Tap once on the cloud icon next to an item to download it again.

To create a playlist of songs, tap once on the **Playlists** button in the left-hand sidebar,

Playlists

then tap once on the **New Playlist** button. Give it a name, and then you can add songs from your Library.

Another music option is Apple Music. This is a subscription service that makes the entire Apple iTunes Library of music available to users. Music can be streamed over the internet, or downloaded so that you can listen to it when you are offline. Apple Music can be accessed from the **Listen Now** button in the left-hand panel of the Music app.

Playing Music

Once music has been bought from the iTunes Store it can be played on your iPad using the Music app. To do this:

1 Tap once on the **Music** app

2 Tap once on the **Library** button in the left-hand sidebar

Library

3 Select one of the options for viewing items in the Library. This can be **Recently Added**, **Artists**, **Albums**, **Songs** or **Genres**

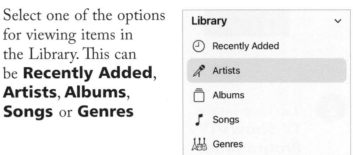

4 For the **Artists** section, tap once on an artist in the left-hand sidebar to view related items in the right-hand panel

5 Tap once on an item in the right-hand panel to view its details. The tracks from the album are displayed

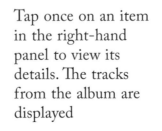

6 Tap once on a track to play it. Limited options for the music controls are displayed at the bottom of the window. Tap once here to view details of a track

7 The details of the track are displayed. Use these buttons to rewind, pause/play and fast-forward the track

8 Tap once on this button to access a menu for the currently-playing track. This includes deleting the track, adding it to a playlist, sharing the song, or adding it as a favorite (**Love**)

Delete from Library 🗑

Download ⊕

Add to a Playlist... ⊞

Share Song... ⬆

Go To Album 🎵

Love ♡

Suggest Less 👎

Don't forget

Tap once on the **Go To Album** option in Step 8 to view a full track listing for the album, as in Step 5 on the previous page.

Taking Photos and Videos

The iPad is excellent for taking and displaying photos. Photos can be captured directly using one of the two built-in cameras (one on the front and one on the back) and then viewed, edited and shared using the Photos app.

 Tap once on the **Camera** app

 Tap once on the shutter button to capture a photo

 Tap once on this button to swap between the front and back cameras on the iPad

Tap once on this button on the top camera toolbar to take a Live Photo, which is a short, animated video in GIF file format. Live Photos can be played in the Photos app by pressing and holding on them to view the animated effects

The main iPad camera can be used for different formats.

 Swipe up or down at the side of the camera screen to access the shooting options. Tap once on the **Photo** button to capture photos at full-screen size. Tap once on the **Square** button to capture photos at this ratio. Tap once on the **Pano** button (accessed by swiping past the **Square** option) to create panoramic shots

Tap once on the **Video** button in Step 1 above, and press the red shutter button to take a video. Press the shutter button again to stop recording

Photos Settings

iCloud sharing

Certain photo options can be applied within Settings. Several of these are to do with storing and sharing your photos via iCloud. To access these:

1 Tap once on the **Settings** app

2 Tap once on the **Photos** tab

3 Drag the **iCloud Photos** button **On**

iCloud Photos

to upload your whole photo library from your iPad to iCloud (it remains on your iPad too). Similarly, photos on your other Apple devices can also be uploaded to iCloud

4 Select an option for storing iCloud photos

Optimize iPad Storage	✓
Download and Keep Originals	

(**Optimize iPad Storage** uses less storage as it uses smaller file sizes of your images on your iPad, although the original file sizes are retained in iCloud)

5 Drag the **Shared Albums**

Shared Albums

button **On** to enable sharing your albums with family and friends, and also to be able to see their shared albums

6 Tap once on the **Shared Library** option to set up a shared photo library for family and friends, as shown on pages 64-65

LIBRARY

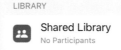
Shared Library
No Participants

In the **Camera** settings, drag the **Grid** button **On** to place a grid over the screen when you are taking photos with the camera, if required. This can be used to help compose photos by placing subjects using the grid.

Check out these **In Easy Steps** titles to help you take great photos with your iPhone: Smartphone Photography in easy steps and 100 Top Tips – Create Great Photos Using Your Smartphone. Visit www.ineasysteps.com for more details.

Viewing and Editing Photos

Photos section

Photos can be viewed and organized in the Photos app. There are different sections for displaying photos in different ways. All photos can be viewed in the Photos section.

Don't forget

The sidebar contains links to the different sections within the Photos app.

Hot tip

Select a photo (or view it at full size) and tap once on the **Share** button to share it in a variety of ways. These include: messaging; emailing; assigning to a contact in your Contacts app; adding to a note; using as your iPad wallpaper; sending to social media; and printing and copying the photo.

 1 Tap once on the **Photos** app

 2 Tap once on this button in the top left-hand corner of the Photos app to show or hide the sidebar

 3 Tap once on the **Library** button in the sidebar and tap once on the **Years**, **Months**, **Days** or **All Photos** buttons to view your photos according to these criteria

 4 In any of the categories, double-tap on a photo to view it at full size

For You section

The **For You** section is where the best of your photos are selected and displayed automatically. To use this:

1 Tap once on the **For You** button on the sidebar

2 The **For You** section contains **Memories**, **Featured Photos**, **Shared with You**, **Shared Albums** and **Sharing Suggestions**

The **Memories** option is an excellent one for viewing slideshows of your best photos, without having to do any of the work of creating them.

3 Memories are collections of photos created by the Photos app, using what it determines are the best shots for a related series of photos

4 Tap once on a slideshow to access control buttons for playing or pausing the slideshow and displaying the photos in a Memory in a grid

...cont'd

My Albums section

Albums can also be created to store similar photos.

1 Access the **My Albums** section within the sidebar

My Albums

☐ All Albums

2 Tap once on the **New Album** button at the bottom of the **My Albums** section

+ New Album

3 Enter a name for the new album and tap once on the **Save** button

New Album
Enter a name for this album.

Winter

Cancel → Save

4 Tap once on the photos to be added to the album, and tap once on the **Add** button in the top right-hand corner of the window

Add

Search options

Items can be searched for in the Photos app by tapping once on the **Search** button in the sidebar. Suggested areas are displayed. Tap once on an item to see the photos within it, or enter a keyword or phrase into the Search box to search for specific items.

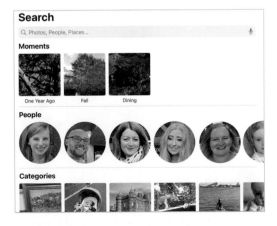

Editing photos

The Photos app has options to perform a range of photo-editing operations. To use these:

1 Open a photo at full-screen size and tap once on the **Edit** button in the top right-hand corner

2 The main editing buttons are located on the left-hand side of the screen. These are for, from top to bottom: color adjustment; filters; and rotation and cropping

3 Tap once on one of the main editing buttons to view its options at the right-hand side of the screen

4 For the **Adjust** options, each item has a slider that can be used to change the level of color adjustment

5 The **Filters** option has a range of filter effects at the right-hand side of the screen. Tap once on one of these to apply it to the photo

6 For the **Crop** option, there are also choices for how to rotate a photo; e.g. horizontally or vertically

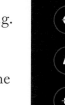

7 Tap once on the **Done** button in the top right-hand corner to apply any editing changes that have been made

Don't forget

The color options in the Adjust section include: **Auto**, **Exposure**, **Brilliance**, **Contrast**, **Brightness**, **Saturation**, and **Tint**.

149

Hot tip

The **Photo Booth** app is a good one to use with grandchildren, who will enjoy experimenting with its fun and special effects. Open the app, select one of the effects, and take a photo as normal.

Reading Books

For anyone interested in reading, the iPad removes the need to carry around a lot of bulky books. Whether you are at home or traveling, you can keep hundreds of digital books (ebooks) on your iPad. This is done with the Books app, which can be used to download and read books across most genres, like a portable library. To use Books:

Hot tip

Tap once on the **Want To Read** button in the sidebar in Step 3 to add a book as a suggested item under the **Reading Now** section.

 Tap once on the **Books** app

Books

 The Books app opens at the **All** section, which consists of any items that you have downloaded, and suggested titles

3 Tap once on the **Book Store** button in the left-hand sidebar to access titles that can be bought and downloaded to the Books app (see the next page)

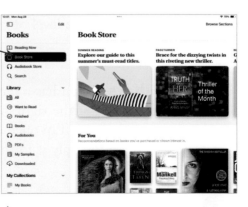

4 Tap once on the **Search** button in the sidebar to view items in the Book Store

Q Search

Once you have identified appropriate books in the Book Store, they can then be downloaded to the **Library** section of the Books app. To do this:

 Tap once on the book image or title to view its details

 View details of the book, including a description. Swipe down the page to view more details about the book

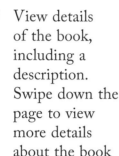

 Tap once on the **Buy** (or **Get**) button to purchase and download the book. Downloaded books appear in the **Library** section of the Books app

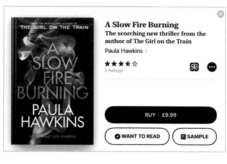

4 Tap once on a book thumbnail in the Library to open it. Tap on the page to access the controls.

Tap once here to move through the book

Hot tip

Tap once on the left-hand and right-hand edges in Step 4 to move back or forward by one page.

Hot tip

Tap once on this button on the bottom toolbar in Step 4 to view the table of contents; options for searching for words or phrases in the book; selecting themes and settings; sharing the book; and bookmarking pages.

Getting the News

The News app is a news-aggregation app that collates news stories from a variety of publications, covering a range of categories. To use the News app:

1 Tap once on the **News** app

2 Tap once on the **Today** button in the sidebar to view current news stories

3 The current news stories, based on your news feed, are displayed in the main window

Tap once on this icon to show or hide the sidebar:

4 Tap once on the **Edit** button to the right of the Search box

5 Your current news feed items can be removed by tapping on the red circle next to them. The order of importance can be rearranged by dragging these buttons. Tap once on the **Done** button at the top of the panel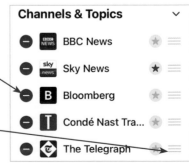

6 Swipe up to the bottom of the left-hand panel, as displayed in Step 3 on the previous page, and tap once on the **Discover Channels** button

Discover Channels

7 Suggested channels and topics are displayed. These can be added to your news feed by tapping once on the **+** icon next to an item. Tap once on the **Done** button in the top right-hand corner

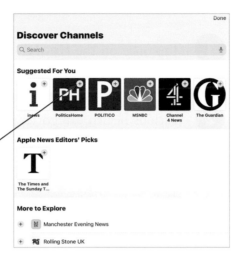

Below the **Channels, Topics & Stories** heading in Step 3 on the previous page is a **Suggested by Siri** heading that contains topics based on Siri searches. Tap once on the **+** icon to add a topic to your news feed.

Hot tip

153

8 Tap once on a news item in Step 3 on the previous page to view it in detail. When an item has been opened for reading, tap on these buttons on the top toolbar to, from left to right: go back to the previous page; bookmark an item; share the current news item; add the item as a favorite, or unfavorite it; change the text size on display; and access a menu

Paris bids adieu to love-or-hate electric scooters

Yann SCHREIBER

© AFP/ALAIN JOCARD
The ban applies to rental scooters

Paris will on Friday become the first European capital to ban floating electric scooters from its streets, leaving fans desolate but relieving those who loathed their "nuisance"

The inclusion of the Health app is a new feature in iPadOS 17.

Tap once on the **Summary** button in the sidebar ♡ Summary at any point to return to this section.

Tap once on the **Show All Health Data** button on the Summary page to view all of the health data that has been added.

 ♥ Show All Health Data

Tap once on this button in the top left-hand corner of the sidebar to show or hide it:

Health App

The Health app has been available on the iPhone for a number of years, and it is now provided on the iPad with iPadOS 17 too. It can be used to collate and display a wide range of health information and also be used in conjunction with an iPhone and an Apple Watch. To use it:

1 Tap once on the **Health** app

2 Various health categories are displayed in the left-hand sidebar, under the **Summary** heading

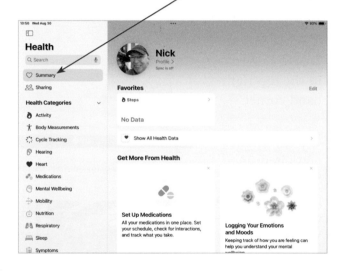

3 Swipe up the Summary page to view the full range of content, including useful health and wellbeing articles

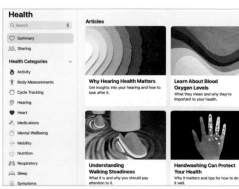

4 Tap once on a category in the left-hand sidebar and tap once on individual items for the category

To synchronize your iPad health data with other devices using the same iCloud account, go to **Settings** > **Apple ID, iCloud, Media & Purchases** > **Apps using iCloud** > **Health** and turn **Sync this iPad** to **On**.

5 Initially, there will be no data, unless it has been synchronized from another device (see the first Hot Tip). Tap once on the **Add Data** button

6 Enter the appropriate data, as required, and tap once on the **Add** button

To add an item as a favorite so that it is displayed on the Summary page, access a main category and select the required item within it. Swipe down to the bottom of the screen and tap once on the **Add to Favorites** star so that it turns solid blue.

7 The data is displayed as a chart for the selected item. Tap once on the **Back** button

8 If an item is a favorite (see the second Hot Tip) it is displayed on the Summary page

Viewing Movies and TV Shows

The TV app can be used to download and view movies and TV shows from the Apple TV service. There is no subscription for using the TV app on the iPad, but individual items usually require a payment to buy or rent them.

Don't forget

If you rent videos from the TV app you have to watch them within 30 days. Once you have started watching a video, you have to finish watching it within 48 hours. Once the rental period has expired, the video is deleted from the iPad.

1 Tap once on the **TV** app

2 The Homepage displays some of the recommended items for the Apple TV+ subscription service

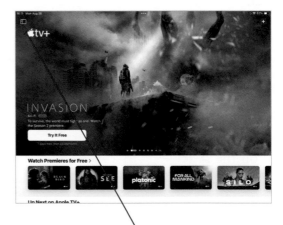

3 Tap once on the **Menu** button to view options for accessing more content

Don't forget

The Apple TV+ service is a subscription service for streaming original TV shows and movies from Apple TV. There is a 7-day free trial and then the service costs $6.99 a month in the US and £8.99 in the UK, at the time of printing.

4 Tap once on the **Watch Now** button to view content suggestions. Tap once on the **Originals** button to view content from the TV+ service. Tap on the **Store** buttons (**Movies** and **TV Shows**) to view more content that can be bought and downloaded. The **Library** option contains downloaded items

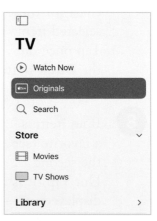

Art and Drawing

Viewing art

It is always a pleasure to view works of art in real life, but the next-best alternative is to be able to look at them on the high-resolution Retina Display on your iPad. As far as viewing art goes, there are two options:

- Using apps that contain general information about museums and art galleries.

- Using apps that display works belonging to museums and art galleries.

In general, type the name of a museum or art gallery into the App Store Search box to see if there is an applicable app.

Creating pictures

If you want to branch out from just looking at works of art, you can try creating some of your own too. There are a range of drawing and painting apps that can be used to let your creative side run riot. Most of these function in a similar fashion in terms of creating pictures, with drawing tools that you can select and then use to create a drawing by using your finger on the screen (or an Apple Pencil). Most drawing apps also have an **Undo** function and an **Eraser** to remove unwanted items. Some apps to try are:

- **Brushes Redux**. One of the most powerful painting apps with a wide range of tools and features, including up to six layers in each painting and five blend modes.

- **Doodle – Drawing Pad**. Similar to Brushes Redux, but not at such a high level.

- **Inspire Pro**. A wide range of blending features makes this one of the best painting apps around.

- **Drawing Desk: Draw & Paint Art**. A drawing app that has tutorials for learning how to draw, and also examples that can be used as templates and copied over.

- **Sketch.Book – Draw, Drawing Pad**. A sketching app at a similar level to Brushes Redux, for painting.

Most top museums have some form of app available. If there is not one for a museum in which you are interested, try contacting the museum and ask if they are planning on developing an app.

If you cannot find a certain app in the search results in the App Store, tap once on the **Filters** button, to the left of the Search box, and select the **Supports > iPhone Only** option. These apps can be downloaded for the iPad too, although they will have a smaller screen area to view the app.

Cooking with your iPad

Your iPad may not be quite clever enough to cook dinner for you, but there are enough cookery apps to ensure that you will never go without a good meal with your iPad at your side. Some to look at are:

- **Allrecipes Magazine**. Packed full of recipes, step-by-step guides and cooking ideas, from the world's largest online community of chefs.

- **BigOven Recipes & Meal Planner**. Over 350,000 recipes to keep you busy in the kitchen for as long as you want. You can also store your grocery lists here.

- **Tasty: Recipes, Cooking Videos**. Over 4,000 new recipes with step-by-step instructions and videos to follow as you create the recipes.

- **Cake Recipes**. To get your mouth watering, this app has hundreds of cake ideas, from the simple to the exotic.

- **Green Kitchen**. A must for vegetarians, with stylish and creative recipes for organic and vegetarian food.

- **Vegan Recipe Club**. An app featuring a comprehensive range of vegan recipes, including options for creating shopping lists and step-by-step guides to preparing tasty vegan meals.

- **Healthy Slow Cooker Recipes & Ingredients**. Put your dish together with this app, leave it in the slow cooker, and then enjoy it several hours later when ready.

Staying Healthy

Most people are more health-conscious these days and, usefully, the App Store has a category covering health and fitness. This includes apps about general fitness, healthy eating, relaxation and yoga. Some to try are:

- **MyFitnessPal: Calorie Counter**. If you want to stick to a diet, this app can help you along the way. You need to register, which is free, and then you can set your own diet plan and fitness profile.

- **Daily Workouts Home Trainer**. Some exercise apps are for dedicated gym-goers. If you are looking for something a bit less extreme, this app could fit the bill, with a range of easy-to-follow exercises that will keep you fit.

- **Yoga for Beginners**. Audio and video instructions to get you started with the benefits of yoga.

- **Simple Meal Planner**. A dieting aid that enables you to create your own menu plans.

- **Pilates Anytime Workout**. Use this app to work through numerous Pilates exercise sessions.

- **Sleep Sounds – Relax & Sleep**. Dozens of different sound files to help you relax or fall asleep. Different melodies can be combined to create a customized soundtrack to help you get to sleep.

- **Pillow: Sleep Tracker**. An app that tracks your sleep, and its quality, to try to ensure that you get the best night's sleep possible.

- **Universal Breathing**. Designed to promote slow breathing, to enhance relaxation and general health.

Don't forget

There is also a **Medical** category in the App Store that contains a range of apps covering varied medical topics and subjects.

Beware

If you have a genuine medical complaint, get it checked out by your doctor, rather than searching online.

As well as the games here, there is a full range of other types of games in the App Store that can be accessed from the **Games** button on the bottom toolbar of the App Store.

For serious game players, the **Arcade** option in the App Store is worth looking at. This is accessed from the bottom toolbar in the App Store, and is a monthly subscription service. It includes all of the latest Apple games, which you can play on your own or against other people, including those in your Family Sharing group.

Playing Games

Although computer games may seem like the preserve of the younger generation, this is definitely not the case. Not all computer games are of the shoot-'em-up or racing variety, and the App Store also contains puzzles and versions of popular board games. Some games to try are:

- **Chess**. Pit your wits against this Chess app. Various settings can be applied for each game, such as the level of difficulty.

- **Checkers**. Similar to the Chess app, but for Checkers (Draughts). Hints are also available to help develop your skills and knowledge.

- **Mahjong**. A version of the popular Chinese game, this is a matching game for single players, rather than playing with other people.

- **Scrabble GO**. An iPad version of the best-selling word game that can be played with up to four people.

- **Solitaire**. An old favorite, the card game where you have to build sequences and remove all of the cards.

- **Sudoku**. The logic game where you have to fill different grids with numbers 1-9, without having any of the same number in a row or column.

- **Tetris**. One of the original computer games, where you have to piece together falling shapes to make lines.

- **Words With Friends**. Similar to Scrabble, an online word game, played with other users.

10 Traveling Companion

This chapter shows how the iPad is an essential travel accessory. It looks at the Maps app for finding locations and getting around, and a range of travel apps.

Beware

To ensure that the Maps app works most effectively, it has to be enabled in Location Services so that it can use your current location (**Settings** > **Privacy & Security** > **Location Services** > **Maps** and select **While Using the App** under **Allow Location Access**).

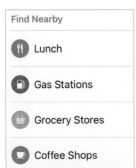

Hot tip

When you tap in the Search box there are options for searching for nearby services, such as restaurants or gas stations. These are relevant to your current location.

Looking Around Maps

With the Maps app you need never again wonder about where a location is, or worry about getting directions to somewhere. As long as you are connected to Wi-Fi or have a 5G/4G/3G network, you will be able to do the following: search maps around the world; find addresses, famous buildings or landmarks; get directions between different locations; and view traffic conditions.

Viewing your current location
To view your current location:

 Tap once on the **Maps** app

 Tap once on this button to view your current location

3 Double-tap on a map with one finger to zoom in (or swipe outward with thumb and forefinger)

4 Tap once with two fingers on a map to zoom out (or pinch inward with thumb and forefinger)

Finding locations
Within Maps you can search for addresses, locations, landmarks or businesses. To do this:

 The Search box is at the bottom of the window. It expands when you tap in it. Enter an item into the Search box. As you type, suggestions appear underneath. Tap on one to go to that location

2 The location is shown on the map, in **Explore** view, and there is information about it in the left-hand panel

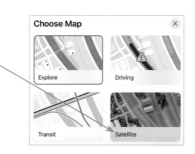

Satellite view
Locations can be viewed in great detail with **Satellite** view.

Hot tip

You can also search for locations by postcode or zip code.

1 In **Explore** view, tap once on this button in the top right-hand corner

2 Tap once on the **Satellite** button

3 A satellite view of the location is displayed. Tap once on the **3D** button to view a graphics-rich 3D view of the location

Don't forget

Some locations provide a 3D Flyover tour. If this is available, a **Flyover** button will be displayed in Step 3.

Getting Directions

Finding your way around is an important element of using maps. This can be done with the **Directions** function.

The Maps app requires an online connection in order to use all of its functionality, either through Wi-Fi or a cellular data connection. However, with iPadOS 17, maps can be downloaded so that they can be viewed when your iPad is offline. To do this, navigate to the required map and tap once on the **Download** button, as in Step 3. This is a new feature in iPadOS 17.

Hot tip

For some destinations alternative routes will be displayed, depending on distance and traffic conditions. Tap on the alternative route to select it, and tap on the **Go** button to proceed.

1 Tap once in the Search box at the top of the window

> Q Loch Ness   ⊗ Cancel
>
> **Loch Ness**
> 73 mi · Lake · Highland, Scotland
>
> **Loch Ness** Centre and Exhibition
> 76 mi · Inverness
>
> **Loch Ness** Monster
> 71 mi · Inverness · Permanently Closed

2 Enter a destination and tap once on one of the results (by default, the directions will be given from your current location)

3 Tap once on this button to get directions for driving

> **Loch Ness** ⬆ ✕
> Lake · Highland, Scotland
>
> 🚗 2h 35m   ⬇ Download   ◉ Website   ··· More
>
> ⬇ **Offline Map of Loch Ness** ✕
> Download an offline map to get around without an internet connection.

4 The route is shown on the map

5 Tap once here in Step 4 to view the route for other transit options. Tap once on the **Now** or **Avoid** button to specify a leaving time and any items to avoid

> **Directions** ✕
>
> 🚗   🚶   🚆   🚲
>
> 📍 My Location
> ⊞ Loch Ness
> ⊕ Add Stop
>
> Now ⌄   Avoid ⌄

6 Tap once on the **Go** button to start the directions and view step-by-step instructions on the map

7 The route is displayed, starting from your current location. Audio instructions tell you the directions to be followed. As you follow the route, the map and instructions are updated

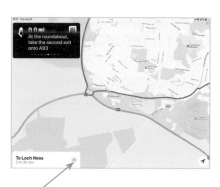

8 Swipe up from here to access **Details** options for the route, which provide a step-by-step view of the route

To get back to the Start view, tap once on the **End Route** button from the box accessed in Step 8.

Driving and Transit views

Two other map views can be used to view driving conditions and available transit options. To use these:

1 Tap once on the **Driving** button in the second Step 2 on page 163 to display a map with traffic conditions such as roadworks and congestion

2 Tap once on the **Transit** button as above to display a map with transit details such as trains, metros and ferries. Tap once on a transit item to view more details in the sidebar

A number of cities have a selection of recommendations available within the Maps app. These are known as Guides and are available for cities including San Francisco, London, New York and Los Angeles. When you search for one of these cities, the Guide will be available in the results.

Traveling with your iPad

When you go traveling, there are a few essentials that you have to consider: passport, money and insurance, to name three. To this you can add your iPad: it is a perfect traveling companion that can help you plan your trip and keep you informed and entertained when you are away from home.

Uses for traveling

There are a lot of App Store apps that can be used for different aspects of traveling. However, the built-in apps can also be put to good use before and during your travels:

166

- **Notes**. Create lists of items to pack or landmarks that you want to visit.

- **Contacts**. Keep your Contacts app up-to-date so that you can use it to send postcards to friends and family. You can also use it to access phone numbers if you want to phone home.

- **Reminders**. Set reminders for important tasks such as changing foreign currency and buying tickets, and for details of flights.

- **Music**. Use this app to play your favorite music while you are traveling or relaxing at your destination.

- **Photos**. Store photos of your trip with this app and play them back as a slideshow when you get home.

- **FaceTime**. If you have a Wi-Fi connection at your destination you will be able to keep in touch using video calls.

- **Books**. Instead of dragging lots of heavy books around, use this app as your vacation library.

Planning your Trip

A lot of the fun and excitement of going on vacation and traveling is in the planning. The anticipation of researching new places to visit and explore can whet the appetite for what is ahead. The good news is, you can plan your whole itinerary while sitting in an armchair with your iPad on your lap. In the App Store there are apps for organizing your itinerary, and others for exploring the possibilities of where you can go, such as:

TripIt

This is an app for keeping all of your travel details in one place. You have to register, which is free, and you can then enter your own itinerary details. Whenever you receive an email confirmation for a flight, hotel or car hire that you have booked, you can email this to your TripIt account and this will be added to your itinerary.

GetPacked

A great way to get peace of mind before you leave. This app generates a packing list and to-do lists to check before you leave, based on questions that you answer about your vacation and travel arrangements. You can then select items to include on your packing list, from clothes to documents and medical items.

Flush Toilet Finder & Map

Perhaps not the most glamorous of apps, but one that can come in very useful. It lists the nearest restrooms/public toilets to your current location, with over 200,000 global options in its database.

World atlas & world map

A comprehensive travel companion that offers a world atlas containing information about countries, cities, landmarks, airports and events. Navigate around the atlas with the same swiping and tapping gestures as the **Maps** app. Tap on an item to access a wealth of information about it.

Although there is a small fee for the **GetPacked** app, it is well worth it, as it covers everything you will need to consider before you leave.

Some map apps are free to download but then there is a fee to buy some of the associated maps.

Viewing Flights

Flying is a common part of modern travel, and although you do not have to book separate flights for a vacation (if it is part of a package) there are a number of apps for booking flights and also following the progress of those in the air, such as:

Skyscanner

This app can be used to find flights at airports around the world. Enter your details such as the departure airport, destination and dates of travel. The results show a range of available options, covering different price ranges.

Flightradar24

If you like viewing the paths of flights that are in the air, or need to check if flights are going to be delayed, this app provides the real-time information you're looking for. Flights are shown according to flight number and airline.

Don't forget

Flight apps need to have an internet connection in order to show real-time flight information.

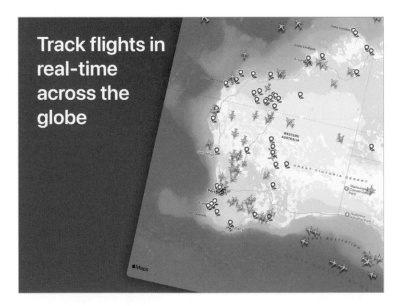

FlightAware Flight Tracker

Another app for tracking flights, showing arrivals and departures, and also information about delays.

Finding Hotels

The internet is a perfect vehicle for finding good-value hotel rooms around the world. When hotels have spare capacity, this can quickly be relayed to associated websites, where users can usually benefit from cheap prices and special offers. There are plenty of apps that have details of thousands of hotels around the world, such as:

Tripadvisor
One of the top travel apps, this not only has hotel information but also restaurants, activities and flights. Enter a destination in the Search box and then navigate through the available options.

When booking flights and hotels, look up the price on your iPad, but check it on other, non-Apple, devices too; e.g. a Windows computer. Sometimes, different prices are displayed for searches from different types of devices.

Hotels.com
A stylish app that enables you to enter search keywords for finding hotels based on destination, hotel name or nearby landmarks.

Booking.com Travel Deals
Another good, fully-featured hotel app that provides a comprehensive service and excellent prices.

lastminute.com
An app that specializes in getting the best prices by dealing with rooms that are available at short notice. Some genuine bargains can be found here, for hotels of all categories.

Most hotel apps have reviews of all of the listed establishments. It is always worth reading these, as it gives you views from people who have actually been there.

Beware

When changing currency, either at home or abroad, always shop around to get the best rate. Using credit cards abroad usually attracts a supplementary charge too.

Hot tip

Some financial/banking apps can be used to convert your local currency to a wide range of global currencies, at the highest exchange rate and with no commission or exchange costs. The app, or physical bank debit card, can then be used to pay for goods and services in the local currency for whichever country you are in. Two to look at are Monza Bank and Revolut.

Converting Currency

Money is always important in life, and never more so than when you are on vacation and possibly following a budget. It is therefore imperative to know the exchange rate of currencies in different countries compared with your own. Two apps that provide this service are:

Xe Currency & Money Transfers

This app delivers information about exchange rates for all major world currencies and also a wealth of background information, such as high and low rates and historical charts.

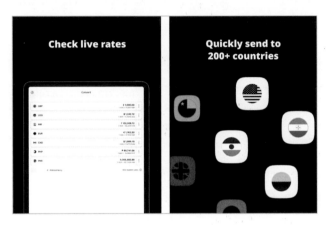

Currency

This app provides up-to-date exchange rates for over 150 currencies and 100 countries.

Travel Apps

Everyone has different priorities and preferences when they are on vacation. The following are some apps from the App Store that cover a range of activities and services:

- **Cities of the World Photo-Quiz**. An app to stimulate your wanderlust, with photo quizzes for recognizing over 110 famous cities. There are different types of quizzes, and also flashcards that provide the answers for you.

- **Disneyland Paris**. If you are entertaining your grandchildren at Disneyland Paris, this app will help you survive the experience. Maps, show times and descriptions of features help you organize all aspects of your visit.

- **Florida State Parks & Areas**. An extensive guide to the outdoor attractions of the Florida State Parks, including general information about all of the parks, advanced GPS maps and a built-in compass.

- **Google Earth**. Not just a travel aid, this app enables you to search the globe and look at photos and 3D maps of all your favorite places.

- **KAYAK**. A useful all-round app that compares hundreds of travel websites to get the best prices for flights, hotels and car rental. You can also create your own itineraries.

- **Language apps**. If you want to learn a new language for your travels, there is a wide range of apps to do this. These are located in either the Travel or Education categories in the App Store.

- **Magnifying Glass with Light**. Not just for traveling, this app acts as a torch and a magnifying glass all in one.

- **National Geographic Traveler**. Subscribe to this app to get an endless supply of high-quality travel features, photography and travel ideas.

- **New York Subway MTA Map**. Use this app to help you get around the Big Apple via the Subway. Plan your journeys and view live updates about stations and routes.

If you cannot find a certain app in the search results in the App Store, tap once on the **Filters** button, to the left of the Search box, and select the **Supports > iPhone Only** option. These apps can be downloaded for the iPad too, although they will have a smaller screen area to view the app.

There are several travel apps that have the functionality to mark locations you have visited around the world. In the **Travel** section of the App Store, enter **places visited** (or similar) into the Search box, to view the matching apps.

...cont'd

The **Phrasebook** app comes with one free language. After that, you have to pay a small fee for each language that you want to use.

Don't forget

There are apps for displaying train times and details, but these are usually specific to your geographical location rather than covering a range of different countries.

- **Paris Travel Guide and Map**. A free map app for travel options around one of the great cities in the world.

- **Phrasebook**. Keep up with what the locals are saying in different countries with this app, which has useful phrases in over 30 languages.

- **Places-Around Me**. Find a variety of different places near to your current location, wherever you are in the world. The app can be used to locate restaurants, hotels, banks, ATMs, and a host of other useful establishments, relative to your current location.

- **Royal Caribbean International**. Find some of your favorite cruises with this app, which displays the full brochure of Royal Caribbean Cruises.

- **SIXT rent share and taxi**. Use this app for car rental, car sharing and taxis in over 100 countries.

- **Translate Free**. If you do not have the time or inclination to learn a new language, try this app to translate over 26 different languages.

- **Tube Map – London Underground**. Find your way around with this digital version of the iconic Tube map. It includes live departure boards and station information.

- **Weather Live**. An app for showing the weather in locations around the world, with graphically-appealing forecasts, including extended forecasts for any coming day of the week or hour.

- **Wi-Fi Connect**. It is always useful to be able to access Wi-Fi when you are on vacation, and sometimes essential. This app locates Wi-Fi hotspots in over two million locations worldwide.

- **Yelp: Local Food & Services**. Covering a range of information, this app locates restaurants, shops, services and places of interest in cities around the world.

11 Practical Matters

This chapter looks at some areas to enable you to have as much peace of mind as possible when using your iPad.

Finding your iPad

No one likes to think the worst, but if your iPad is lost or stolen, help is at hand. The Find My iPad function (operated through the iCloud service) allows you to send a message and an alert to a lost iPad, and also remotely lock it or even wipe its contents. This gives added peace of mind, knowing that even if your iPad is lost or stolen, its contents will not necessarily be compromised. To set up Find My iPad (before it becomes lost or stolen):

Location Services must be turned **On** to enable the Find My iPad service (**Settings** > **Privacy & Security** > **Location Services** and turn **Location Services** to **On**).

1 Tap once on the **Settings** app

2 Tap once on the **Apple ID, iCloud, Media & Purchases** account option

3 Tap once on the **Find My** option

4 Tap once on **Find My iPad** and drag the **Find My iPad** button **On** to be able to find your iPad on a map

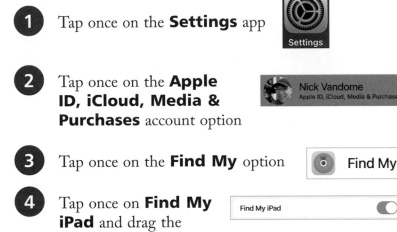

Finding a lost iPad
Once you have set up Find My iPad you can search for it through the iCloud service, using another device. To do this:

Another app that can be used to find a lost device is **Lookout – Mobile Data Security**, which can be downloaded from the App Store.

 Log in to your iCloud account at **www.icloud.com**

 Click once on the **Find My** button

174

...cont'd

3 Click once on the **All Devices** button and select your iPad. It is identified, and its current location is displayed on the map

4 Click once on a green dot to view details about when your iPad was located (each green dot represents a different device). Click once on the **i** symbol to view more information about your iPad

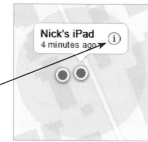

5 Click once here to send a sound alert to your iPad. This can be useful if you have lost it in the house or close by

6 Click once here to lock your iPad

7 Enter a message that will appear on the iPad. Its existing 6-digit passcode will then be required to unlock it (if it does not have one, you will be prompted to add one)

Click once on the **Erase iPad** button in Step 5 to delete the iPad's contents. It is extremely important to have previously backed up your iPad content using iCloud (**Settings** > **Apple ID, iCloud, Media & Purchases** > **iCloud** > **iCloud Backup** and turn the **Back Up This iPad** option **On**) so that you can restore the content to a new device, or your original one if it is found.

If you are using Family Sharing (see pages 67-70) you can use the **Find My** app to locate the devices of other Family Sharing members.

Malware is short for malicious software, designed to harm your computer, or access and distribute information from it.

Apple also checks apps that are provided through the App Store, and this process is very robust. This does not mean that it is impossible for a virus to infect the iPad, so keep an eye on the Apple website to see if there are any details about iPad viruses.

Check out 100 Top Tips – Stay Safe Online and Protect Your Privacy at www. ineasysteps.com for more help with keeping your online data safe and secure.

Avoiding Viruses

As far as security from viruses on the iPad is concerned, there is good news and bad news:

- The good news is that due to its architecture, most apps on the iPad do not communicate with each other, so even if there were a virus, it is unlikely that it would infect the whole iPad. Also, there are relatively few viruses being aimed at the iPad, particularly compared with those for Windows PCs.

- The bad news is that no computer system is immune from viruses and malware, and complacency is one of the biggest enemies of computer security. There have been some instances of photos in iCloud being accessed and hacked, but this was more to do with password security – or lack of – rather than viruses.

iPad security
Apple takes security on the iPad very seriously, and one way that this manifests itself is in the fact it is designed so that different apps do not talk to each other. This means that if there were a virus in an app, it would be hard for it to transfer to other apps and therefore spread across the iPad. Apple checks apps very rigorously, but even this is not foolproof, as shown in various attacks that have taken place against Apple devices.

Antivirus options
There are a few apps in the App Store that deal with antivirus issues, but do not actually remove viruses:

- **McAfee**. The online security firm has a number of apps that cover issues such as privacy of data and password security.

- **Norton**. Another popular online security option that has a range of apps to check for viruses and malware.

- **F-Secure: Total Security & VPN**. This can be used for complete online protection for mobile devices and your data, privacy and identity.

Privacy

The Privacy settings contain options for limiting how your apps use your location and also provide a report of app activity on your iPad. To use the Privacy settings:

1 Open the Settings app and tap once on the **Privacy & Security** tab

 Privacy & Security

2 Tap once on the **Location Services** option and turn it **On** to specify which apps can, and cannot, access your location. Tap once on the **Tracking** option to specify whether websites have to ask before they track your online activities (see the Hot tip)

Location Services	Off >
Tracking	>
Contacts	>
Calendars	>
Reminders	>
Photos	>

Hot tip

For the **Tracking** option in Step 2, drag the **Allow Apps to Request to Track** option **On** to ensure that apps have to ask for permission to track your activities. When this request is made you can decline permission for the app to track your activities.

< Privacy & Security **Tracking**

Allow Apps to Request to Track

177

3 At the bottom of the **Privacy** window, tap once on the **App Privacy Report** button

App Privacy Report

4 Tap once on the **Turn On App Privacy Report** option to view details for relevant items

< Privacy & Security **App Privacy Report**

App Privacy Report

App Privacy Report shows how often apps use the permission you've granted to access your data, like your location or microphone. It also includes a breakdown of each app's network activity, website network activity, and the most frequently contacted domains.

Learn more...

Turn On App Privacy Report

Screen Time

The amount of time that we spend on our digital devices is a growing issue in society, and steps are being taken to let us see exactly how much time we are spending looking at our mobile screens. In iPadOS 17, a range of screen-use options can be monitored with the Screen Time feature. To use this:

Hot tip

Once **App & Website Activity** has been turned **On**, it can be turned **Off** again by tapping once on the **Turn Off App & Website Activity** button at the bottom of the main **Screen Time** window in Step 3.

Turn Off App & Website Activity

Don't forget

Each week, the **Screen Time** option produces a report based on the overall usage, as shown in Step 3. The report is identified with a notification when it is published each week.

1 Select **Settings** > **Screen Time**   ⧗ Screen Time

2 Options for using **Screen Time** are displayed. Tap once on the **App & Website Activity** option and tap once on the **Turn On App & Website Activity** button on the next screen

Turn On App & Website Activity

3 A graph of your screen usage is displayed, along with more Screen Time options (see the next page). Tap once on the **See All App & Website Activity** option to see a full breakdown of your screen usage. The full range of Screen Time options is listed below the graph – see pages 179-180

Options for Screen Time

On the Screen Time settings page, in Step 3 on the previous page, there are options for viewing apps and content.

1 Tap once on **Downtime**

Downtime
Schedule time away from the screen

2 Tap once on the **Turn On Downtime Until Schedule** button **On**, then turn the **Scheduled** button **On** and tap once on the options for when only specified apps are available

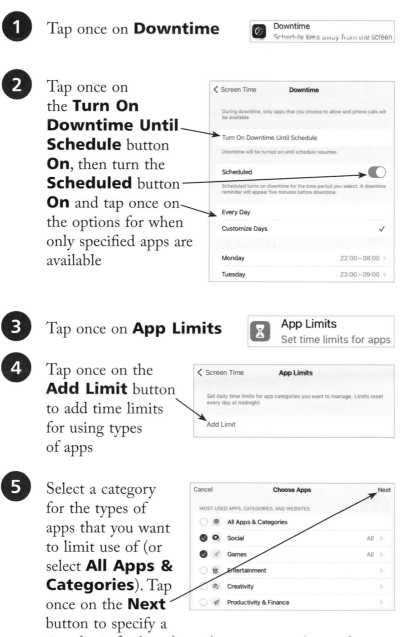

3 Tap once on **App Limits**

App Limits
Set time limits for apps

4 Tap once on the **Add Limit** button to add time limits for using types of apps

5 Select a category for the types of apps that you want to limit use of (or select **All Apps & Categories**). Tap once on the **Next** button to specify a time limit for how long these apps can be used

Tap once on the **Screen Distance** button in Step 3 on the previous page to activate an alert for when you have been holding your iPhone's screen too close for an extended period of time. This is a new feature in iPadOS 17.

Screen Distance
Reduce eye strain

Tap once on the **Lock Screen Time Settings** option further down the screen in Step 3 on the previous page to create a Screen Time passcode, for locking the Screen Time settings. The passcode can be used to allow more time when any limits have been reached.

Lock Screen Time Settings

...cont'd

6 Tap once on **Always Allowed**

Always Allowed
Choose apps to allow at all times

7 The apps that are always allowed to operate, regardless of what settings there are for Screen Time, are displayed. Tap once on the red circle next to one to remove it. Select items below the **Choose Apps** heading (further down the window) to add more

< Screen Time   Always Allowed

ALLOWED CONTACTS
Limit who you can communicate with during downtime. Limits apply to Phone, FaceTime, Messages, and iCloud contacts.

Contacts   Everyone >

ALLOWED APPS
Always allowed apps are available during downtime, or if you selected the "All Apps & Categories" app limit.

- Phone
- Messages
- FaceTime
- Maps

8 Tap once on **Communication Limits**

Communication Limits
Set limits based on contacts

9 Tap once on **During Screen Time** or **During Downtime** to limit who can contact you, and communicate with you, during these times

< Screen Time   Communication Limits

Limits apply to Phone, FaceTime, Messages, and iCloud contacts. Communication to known emergency numbers identified by your carrier is always allowed.

ALLOWED COMMUNICATION

During Screen Time   >
Everyone

Limit who you can communicate with during allowed screen time.

During Downtime   >
Everyone

10 Tap once on **Content & Privacy Restrictions**

Content & Privacy Restrictions
Block inappropriate content

11 Drag the **Content & Privacy Restrictions** button **On** to apply restrictions for blocking inappropriate content

< Back   Content & Privacy Restrictions

Content & Privacy Restrictions   ⬤

iTunes & App Store Purchases   >
Allowed Apps   >
Content Restrictions   >

The options for allowing communications in Step 9 are: **Contacts Only**; **Contacts & Groups with at Least One Contact**; or **Everyone**.

< Back   During Screen Time

Limits apply to Phone, FaceTime, Messages, and iCloud contacts. Communication to known emergency numbers identified by your carrier is always allowed.

ALLOWED COMMUNICATION

Contacts Only

Contacts & Groups with at Least One Contact

Everyone   ✓

Another communication option within Screen Time is **Communication Safety**. This can be used to filter out inappropriate content in photos or videos that are sent to you.

 Communication Safety
Protect from sensitive content

Updating Software

The operating system that powers the iPad is known as iPadOS. This is a mobile-computing operating system that is specifically tailored to the iPad. The latest version is iPadOS 17. Periodically, there are updates to iPadOS to fix bugs and add new features. These can be downloaded to your iPad once they are released.

If your iPadOS software is up-to-date, there is a message to this effect in the **Software Update** window.

1 Tap once on the **Settings** app

2 Tap on the **General** tab | General

3 Tap on the **Software Update** option

Software Update	>

Software Update can be set to be performed automatically overnight, when the iPad is charging and connected to Wi-Fi. To do this, tap on the **Automatic Updates** button in Step 4 and drag the **iPadOS Updates** button **On** to download updates automatically.

4 If there is an update available (or a new version of iPadOS) it will be displayed here, with details of what is contained within it, from this link

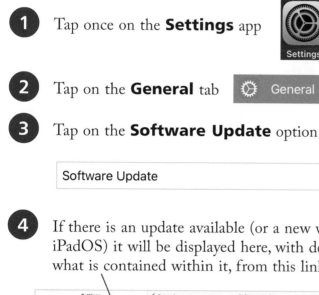

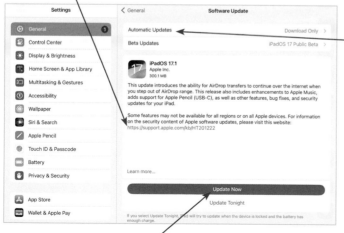

5 Tap once on the **Update Now** button to start the download process. The iPadOS update will then download and install automatically

Accessibility Issues

The iPad tries to cater to as wide a range of users as possible, including those who have difficulty with vision or hearing, or those with physical and motor issues. There are a number of settings that can help with these areas. To access the range of accessibility settings:

1 Tap once on the **Settings** app

2 Tap on the **Accessibility** tab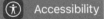

3 The settings for **Vision**, **Physical and Motor**, **Hearing** and **General** are displayed here

In the **Accessibility > Display & Text Size** section, drag the **On/Off Labels** button **On** to display an extra graphical symbol on the **On/Off** buttons, to further help identify their state.

Accessibility

VISION

VoiceOver	Off >
Zoom	Off >
Hover Text	Off >
AA Display & Text Size	>
Motion	>
Spoken Content	>
Audio Descriptions	Off >

PHYSICAL AND MOTOR

Touch	>
Switch Control	Off >
Voice Control	Off >
Home Button	>
Apple TV Remote	>
Keyboards	>

Vision settings
These can help anyone with impaired vision, and there are options to hear items on the screen and also for making text easier to read.

1 Tap once on the **VoiceOver** option

VISION		
VoiceOver		Off >

2 Drag this button **On** to activate the VoiceOver function. This then enables items to be spoken when you tap on them

< Accessibility   **VoiceOver**

VoiceOver

VoiceOver speaks items on the screen:
· Tap once to select an item.
· Double-tap to activate the selected item.
Learn more...

VoiceOver Practice

When VoiceOver is **On**, tap once on an item to select it and have it spoken; double-tap to activate the item.

183

3 Select options for VoiceOver, as required

SPEAKING RATE

Speech	>
Braille	>
VoiceOver Recognition	>
Verbosity	>
Audio	>

There is a wide range of options for the way VoiceOver can be used. For full details, see the Apple website at **https://www.apple.com/accessibility/vision/**

If you turn on the **Zoom** function, you can magnify areas of the screen with a magnification window. To activate this, double-tap with three fingers. Drag with three fingers within the window to view different areas of the screen, or press and hold on the tab in the middle bottom of the window to drag it into different positions.

...cont'd

4 Tap once on the **Accessibility** button to return to the main options

< Accessibility

5 Tap once on these options to access settings for zooming or magnifying the screen, and increasing the text size

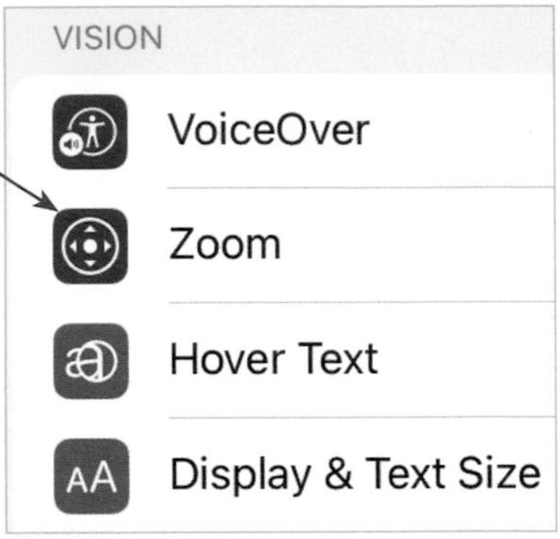

VISION

VoiceOver

Zoom

Hover Text

AA Display & Text Size

6 Tap again on the **Accessibility** button to return to the main options after each selection

Hearing settings
These can be used to change the iPad speaker from stereo to mono. To do this:

1 Tap once on the **Audio & Visual** button in the **Hearing** section and drag this button **On** to enable **Mono Audio**

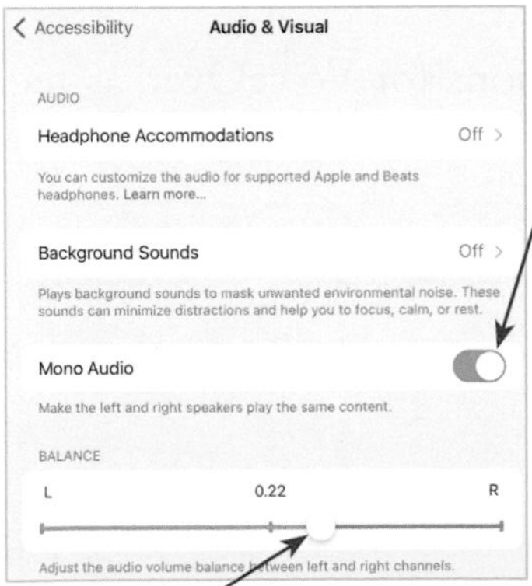

< Accessibility   Audio & Visual

AUDIO

Headphone Accommodations   Off >

You can customize the audio for supported Apple and Beats headphones. Learn more...

Background Sounds   Off >

Plays background sounds to mask unwanted environmental noise. These sounds can minimize distractions and help you to focus, calm, or rest.

Mono Audio

Make the left and right speakers play the same content.

BALANCE

L   0.22   R

Adjust the audio volume balance between left and right channels.

2 Drag this button to specify whether sound comes out of the left or right speaker

AssistiveTouch

This can be used by anyone who has difficulty navigating around the iPad with the screen or buttons. It can be used with an external device such as a joystick, or it can be used on its own. To use AssistiveTouch (under **Physical and Motor > Touch**):

1 Tap once on the **AssistiveTouch** option

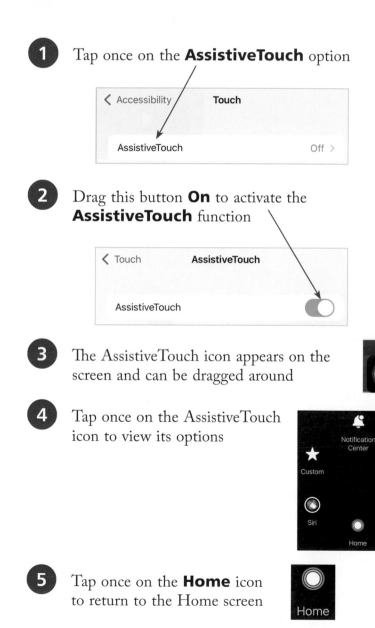

2 Drag this button **On** to activate the **AssistiveTouch** function

3 The AssistiveTouch icon appears on the screen and can be dragged around

4 Tap once on the AssistiveTouch icon to view its options

5 Tap once on the **Home** icon to return to the Home screen

185

The **AssistiveTouch** options make it easier for anyone with difficulties clicking the **Home** button, or using Multitasking Gestures, for iPads that use a **Home** button.

The AssistiveTouch **Home** button option can be used if the physical **Home** button is ever damaged or does not work, for iPads that use a **Home** button.

...cont'd

6 Tap on the **Device** icon in Step 4 on page 185

Device

7 Tap once to activate the required function, including changing the screen rotation and adjusting the volume

Tap on the **More** button in the **Device** window to select options for creating more gestures, shaking the iPad, capturing a screenshot, and accessing the **App Switcher** window.

Guided Access

The Guided Access option allows for certain functionality within an app to be disabled so that individual tasks can be focused on without any other distractions. To use this:

1 Under the **General** heading, tap once on the **Guided Access** option

GENERAL

Guided Access

2 Drag this button **On** to activate the Guided Access functionality

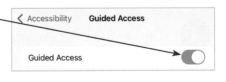

Hot tip

For iPads with no **Home** button, activate Guided Access by triple-clicking the **Lock** button on the side of the iPad.

3 Open an app, and triple-click on the **Home** button to activate Guided Access within the app

4 Circle an area on the screen to disable it (this can be any functionality within the app). Tap on the **Start** button to activate Guided Access for that area. The circled area will not function within the app

Index

Q

R

S